Ph.D. War Stories

Real People ~ Real Stories ~ Real Success

Edited By

GEORGE W. RIDEOUT, D.B.A.

Dedication

To those who chase their dreams and never accept defeat....

Contents

Foreword

The decision to pursue a terminal degree represents a life-changing commitment. Successfully completing a doctoral program is a rewarding but eye-opening experience. As a student, you are pushed to the limits and forced to make tough choices. Do I spend valuable time with family and friends, or do I study? Do I give up hobbies and make the conscious decision to hole up in a room alone for hours every day for perhaps three or more years? Did you know that research shows the average time to complete a doctoral degree is more than seven years, and most either quit or finish all but dissertation (ABD)?

A fellow student likened completing a doctorate to boot camp for Marines: grueling, intimidating, and causing you to question your own reasons for making the decision to do this. Although not physical, the challenges are similar, requiring every student to commit to a higher ideal in not only themselves but also their peers. Anyone who has attended or completed a doctoral program understands the phrase "not for the faint of heart."

In this book, you will read the stories of people who made this commitment. The stories are the authors' personal reflections about how they achieved their degree or are surviving the grind of a program. You will read about trials and tribulations and also success. Perhaps more important, this book is about real life. The authors are you! From overcoming health issues to family tragedy to fighting a war, their stories run the gamut of challenges that most would find overwhelming when trying to enter or complete the rigors of a doctoral program. If you are a current learner, their stories will inspire you to keep moving forward regardless of your situation. If you are thinking about becoming a doctoral student, their stories can rally you to join the ranks. Finally if you have achieved your doctorate, the stories will fill you with pride and cause you to reflect on your own journey.

Ph.D. War Stories is dedicated to everyone who has made the decision to pursue higher education, specifically a terminal degree. Although the title says "Ph.D.," the book is for anyone in a doctoral program. If you accept this challenge, I applaud your commitment not only to yourself and your future, but also to higher education and setting an example for others. I also applaud the *Ph.D. War*

Stories authors. Your willingness to share your personal memoirs is an invaluable service. You give proof that the doctoral mountain is not insurmountable! You are an inspiration!

---*George W. Rideout*

Ph.D. War Stories
Real People ~ Real Stories ~ Real Success

1 Achieving My Doctorate: A Journey of a Lifetime

Rose Marie Balan

On the side of my desk a large diploma rests against the wall. I haven't yet found the ideal spot for mounting it; hence, it sits very close to me where I can glance across and reminisce about all that this degree has meant. In its elegant frame of maroon and gold, the diploma is tangible proof of the journey I have recently completed. This journey was among the most rewarding and life-changing experiences I have had thus far.

Comparing the doctoral process to a journey is fitting. Imagine a long distance cross-country trip involving steep hills, deep valleys, switchbacks, rough washboard roads and the occasional smooth highway. In many respects my doctoral journey was like that trip. Sometimes the sheer effort involved was like climbing the steepest hill, the frustration was like descending into the deepest valley, and the halting progress was like making two steps forward and one step back. Through perseverance I forged ahead no matter how difficult the situation became. I am of the opinion that if I can do this, then anyone can.

The decision to begin the doctoral program came as a result of my success in the master's program. With my bachelor's degree I have been a classroom teacher since 1976. Because of living in a small city without a university campus, opportunities for continued studies were somewhat limited, but I have always harbored a strong desire to further my education. An Internet search in 2002 informed me that opportunities existed for on-line master's degree programs. After weighing the pros and cons of enrolling in an on-line program, I decided the benefits outweighed the risks, and sent in my application. In my 50s I would undertake a journey that had life-changing implications.

After being out of the classroom for almost 20 years the transition to being a student was challenging and somewhat daunting. The first course in my master's program was qualitative research methods. The text used for that course contained particularly dense scholarly language. To fully comprehend the text, I needed to sit with a dictionary, the textbook, and a notebook as I translated and paraphrased the text into language that I could comprehend. What exactly was epistemology, ontology, or methodology? I was soon to find out.

From the beginning, my re-entry into scholarship was plagued by personal struggles. Prior to beginning the first course, I fell and the resulting fracture to my right *humerus* meant that my arm was immobilized for most of three months. Although typing one-handed, I was able to complete my first and subsequent courses with good results. Unfortunately, the next year I had a similar fracture in the other arm, my left. Since I am left hand-dominant I was once again typing one-handedly but this time with the added difficulty of having to rely on my non-dominant side.

My commitment and dedication to advancing myself personally and professionally served me well as I continued throughout the two-year program. At one point a dog bite I had received while taking bottles and cans to the recycling depot went septic. The result of the infection was that I was once again on medical leave from my job and had to go to the hospital for IV antibiotics every eight hours for several days. In the final year of the master's program my physical struggles continued as I developed deep vein thrombosis (DVT). Finally, in spite of these personal challenges, my coursework was completed and I was able to graduate from the master's program and receive my diploma.

The abrupt end of my studies left me with idle hands and empty evenings as I looked for things to do. As a result of my teaching job my days were full, but the evenings were less fulfilling. Where once I was busy and feeling a sense of fulfillment as assignments and courses were completed, now the evenings seemed purposeless. I loved conducting research, but without a focus, that research was purposeless. I was restless; I was not yet ready to stop learning. The learning bug had bitten me, and I wanted more. My commitment to lifelong learning had been intensified. I was encouraged by the remembrance that certain professors from the master's program had recommended me for their doctoral program. Unfortunately, my research interests were outside of the scope of that university, and I needed to consider other options. After only a few months off, I applied to and was accepted by the University of Phoenix (UOP).

The transition from master's to doctoral program and from one university to another was seamless. The coursework I had completed meshed well with the new courses I was yet to take. The

4

fact that I had completed the master's program from one country and was continuing in the doctoral program from another made no difference. I was even able to use some of the same text materials. Once again I felt a sense of purpose when I came home each evening, and once again I felt the sense of fulfillment as I completed my assignments and eventually my courses. I wish I could say the learning and the professional growth I was making with each course completed solely motivated me. Realistically though, I was as motivated by the A's I received as any first grader is from receiving a gold star. The added impetus for achieving good grades came through the other students in my cohort. I was blessed to be in a cohort of high achievers for whom doing well was important and for whom nothing less than an A would be acceptable. The bar was set high, and I felt the need to work hard to reach the personal goals I had set and to keep up with the other students in the program, some of whom were to become my dear friends.

One benefit of the structure of the UOP program is that each summer short residencies are held to allow students to meet face-to-face to participate in intense coursework that leads to the dissertation. My first residency was held in Baltimore, Maryland. It seemed as if several hundred students were at this residency, the added bonus of which was that I could finally meet the students from my cohort. While the days and much of the evenings were filled with assignments and projects, time was still available for dinners out, trips to the inner harbor, and fun. One of the main assignments for residency participants was to complete a project together in a format similar to Donald Trump's television program "The Apprentice." Students were divided into groups, with each group member having a specific role, and each group having a project manager. Tension was high as six individuals from very diverse backgrounds attempted to work in harmony to achieve the desired result. Achieving unity meant compromise, a practice that was not always easy. The second and third residencies were in Arlington, Virginia. Once again, the time spent was very intense. Days were long and tiring, and fulfillment came as a result of much blood, sweat, and tears to complete the requirements of the program.

I always maintained that the setting for the residencies did not matter that much. One could be situated in Timbuktu for all it mattered, given our long hours of study and little opportunity for sightseeing, but that is not really true. I always scheduled an extra day or two at the residency sites so that it would feel like I had a mini-vacation. The days were long and often we were up until well into the wee hours to complete assignments before their deadline. I remember being up until after four in the morning prior to the last day of class in year-one residency, but some students did not make it to bed at all. Opportunities for socialization were special; a deep bond had been forged between classmates. This bond was strengthened by the challenges that students faced together. I know that at least two other women from my cohort and I will be lifelong friends.

Following the year-two residency, little time was available to recharge one's batteries; students were required to complete several statistical modules prior to beginning the quantitative research course. I spent most of that two-week break working on statistics. Never being particularly astute at math, statistics seemed especially challenging. A deadline loomed. All the modules needed to be completed. To me, it seemed like a great deal of work was accomplished, but little progress was made. Sometimes, I needed to do the same module over several times before I understood what I was doing. In spite of the frustration, completing those modules gave me a profound sense of accomplishment. Their completion was one of the more challenging aspects of the program.

During the year-three residency, in our first short course, students were required to complete increasingly more complex projects in larger and larger groups culminating in a whole-group presentation to the United Nations based on the global water shortage. Each individual or group was given a particular task assuming the roles of writers, audio-video support, researchers, and producers. My role became that of presenter, and it was my job to describe the current global water crisis and ask the United Nations for support. Although our instructor assumed the role of the entire United Nations, we approached the task with all the intensity that would be expected if the situation were real rather than a mock-up. I remember the tension I felt as I started my part of the presentation and the relief that was felt when it was over. To this day whenever I am faced with a difficult task, I remind myself that I had successfully presented to the "United Nations."

The workload for the doctoral program was at first very intense, and students needed to make substantive posts on five out of seven days and still do major individual and group papers. In addition to the academic work, students faced the rigors of dealing with family life, jobs, the extended family, and all the other challenges of life. Although I had not married, family life was very important to me. My mother and two sisters and their families and I maintained a very close relationship.

In the spring of 2008, one of my two sisters became gravely ill with pneumonia. She was in our local hospital for two weeks prior to her release. Unfortunately, she was not better. After being home for only a matter of a few days, she was sent by air ambulance to a larger hospital in Vancouver. Instead of improving, her condition deteriorated to the point where she lost the ability to swallow or speak. She was on the ventilator for most of the two months of her hospitalization. Her pneumonia became resistant to most of the antibiotics offered, and she passed away in August of 2011.

The only way I was able to concentrate during those days was through compartmentalization. While at work, I tried to focus only on the challenges of the school day. While doing my assignments I tried, as much as I could, to focus only on my studies.

From the first moment I saw the various tubes and machines that were keeping her alive, I knew my sister would not survive. Emotionally, I was in denial and believed a way existed for her to overcome this disease and get better. The dichotomy between what I could see and understand intellectually and what I felt with my heart created discord that caused much internal turmoil; my feelings alternated between hope and despair. Having to keep up with the coursework provided me with an outlet whereby I could channel my energies and focus my thoughts so that I would not dwell on the inevitable. The week after my sister's funeral I flew to Arlington, Virginia, for the final residency. The busyness of that residency prevented me from sinking into a spiral of depression following her passing.

Throughout the coursework part of the doctoral program, the members of my cohort and I supported each other with challenges of the program and of life. Feedback from the instructors was quick. Camaraderie grew from being in a course with a group of people, even though the class members were spread across the US and Canada. The timeline of the courses was such that we had almost daily contact with each other. That was all to change once the coursework had been completed, and we each worked on our dissertations.

Writing a dissertation is a lonely and frustrating preoccupation. Challenges occur for a variety of reasons. Contact with the mentor is somewhat limited, through no fault of the mentors. The mentors still have courses to teach and family life to live in addition to helping students with their dissertations. At times, lengthy sections need to be rewritten if we have gone astray. I was fortunate; my relationship with my mentor was good, and she was able to steer me in the right direction before I had gone too much off course. Research participants do not come easy, and long periods of time can go by between participant interviews. Processing the results of the study is tedious and requires that the researcher evaluate and re-evaluate the data again. Using research software presents a new set of challenges. Time does not allow for learning and fully understanding the program; therefore, using such programs does not help as much as it could. Writing a dissertation requires acceptance from two university panels. Waiting for feedback from these boards can be nerve-wracking. The dissertation phase is that part of the journey that challenges and puts to use all the skills the student has learned along the way, yet the student is travelling without a roadmap.

I would like to say that my physical challenges ended after the completion of my master's program, but that was not the case. In some respects, my earlier challenges seemed like a dress rehearsal for what was to come. At the age of 15, I was diagnosed with juvenile rheumatoid arthritis. The treatment protocol at that time was for the least aggressive medications to be tried first, gradually working up to the harder drugs because of their potential for adverse side effects. Medications of the 70s and 80s may have controlled pain to a degree but did little to prevent joint damage. For that reason, I had a great deal of joint damage while still at a relatively young age. I required my first knee replacement when I was 25, followed by a total hip replacement, replacement of the other knee, and a revision of the first knee surgery. Those surgeries improved the quality of my life significantly and enabled me to live a near-normal life. The longevity of replaced joints is typically about 10-15 years. I was fortunate in that mine lasted much longer.

At about the time I enrolled in the doctoral program, I experienced increasingly severe pain and stiffness in my feet and ankles and was referred to a foot surgeon. The surgeon noticed a profound instability in my knee, and informed me that I would need a revision of my knee surgery before he could proceed with the feet and ankle reconstruction. At the first visit with a general orthopedic surgeon, I found out I would require revisions to both my hip and knee. What would have been one procedure ended up being many more. I had my left knee revision in the fall of 2008, the left hip surgery in the summer of 2009, right elbow joint replacement in September of 2010, left elbow joint replacement in March of 2011, left elbow tendon repair in May of 2011, and right knee revision surgery in August 2011. While many of these surgeries occurred after the completion of my doctoral program, the implications of my needing them were very much present throughout the time I was working toward my degree.

The date of the oral defense for my dissertation holds great significance for me. I remember the anxiety I felt prior to the defense, which was conducted via a conference call. My committee members were from various areas of the US and Canada, but through technology we were able to meet. Even though no one could see me, I prepared for my defense by dressing in my best clothing, carefully applying my make-up, and physically doing all I could to make me feel my best. The defense went well; I had rehearsed several times so that my presentation would go off without a hitch. As required by the university, I left the call early to allow my committee members the opportunity to discuss my presentation and dissertation. Since my part had been completed, I went to school to have lunch with my colleagues. Still feeling euphoric, I shared with them the highlights of my experience. As I took a bite of my apple, my elbow snapped and my arm fell to the table. I tried to lift my arm, but it would not move. I had every intention of teaching class that afternoon, but when I stood up, I became very pale and it became clear to others that something was very wrong. My colleagues urged me to go to the emergency room to determine what was going on. The outcome of that visit was that I would need to be off work for three months and would require elbow joint replacement surgery. My elbow was fractured and, because of the damage from the rheumatoid arthritis, required replacement. The problem was I had already been waiting for surgery for my left elbow. Until I regained some mobility in the right arm, I basically had two non-functioning arms. X-rays later

14

confirmed that both elbow joints were fractured, but neither fracture healed prior to the elbow joint replacement surgery. While I could still type to a limited degree, I needed to use a straw to drink and long-handled utensils in order to eat or perform my self-care. Fortunately only a very few minor adjustments were necessary to my dissertation following my oral defense so there was no need for me to challenge the limited use I had of my arms at that time. Finally, in spite of the many hurdles along the way I was given notice that the dean had approved my dissertation, and I was now officially a doctor.

Along with many thousands of other graduates, I had the privilege of walking across the stage and being hooded on July 23, 2011. In awe I looked across the UOP stadium at the many people also graduating that day, and wondered what I was doing there. Listening to Tom Brokaw deliver his address seemed even more surreal; I had only seen him on television, never imagining I would see him in the flesh. Listening to Patricia Igbinovia, our 72-year-old Nigerian valedictorian who had done so much to improve educational opportunities in her country, made me realize how much potential each of us has for achieving greatness. I also was filled with the awareness that all of my personal struggles leading up to that day had been worth it. At last I felt like a doctor. The challenge now will be to put that learning to good use, to share what I have learned. Achieving the doctorate is not the end of my journey, but rather the doctorate provides the means whereby I can go forward and continue to meet new personal and professional goals.

2 A Doctorate? Why?
Edith Caldwell

There may be various psychological reasons why I decided to pursue a doctoral degree, but as I think about it, it is not that complex or involved. Originally, I had not planned on going beyond my associate of arts degree when I started higher education in 1972. Twenty years later, I still had not obtained the two-year degree in computer studies. Due to my boss' encouragement and a scholarship for $ 800, I returned to school, and in 1997, I received an associate of arts in applied business with a concentration in computer studies. At age 40, I considered myself done.

Fifteen years later, my daughter suggested I go to school and get a bachelor's degree, but I felt I was too old. After further persuasion from my daughter-in-law, too, I did return to school and received a bachelor in computer science. I realized after being in the discipline, life in school was more challenging than I expected. I promised to quit after each class, but I didn't. Surprisingly, I graduated with a decent GPA of 3.77. In our last class, the professor suggested we take off a year or two before deciding to go on for our master's degrees. I thought to myself, I'm too old to wait a year or two; I'd better get this done, now! So, after getting my bachelor's degree, I went for the master's program, receiving a master in organized management, earning a GPA of 3.92. I couldn't believe it!

While I was in the master's program, an old acquaintance told me about the PhD Project. The PhD Project supports minorities of all kinds to go after and obtain a doctorate in order to help others of their culture in furthering their education. The PhD Project is sponsored by the KPMG Foundation and supports both those interested in becoming doctors and those who already have become doctors. After becoming part of the PhD Project, I was convinced I should continue my education to as high as I could go.

At age 60, I entered the doctoral program at the University of Phoenix in educational leadership, specializing in educational technology. Today, I am working on a dissertation about individuals 65 to 75 and their relationship with employment. Older adults are vital to our society and even to us personally. They should be encouraged to pursue their education and continue working if they desire. Older adults share the same goals and objectives as younger people, although their scope may be more limited. My desire is to be part of changing negative attitudes toward older adults. My passion is teaching, so I want to teach — especially older adults. In addition, I would like to be an advocate for older adults.

So, my catalysts for pursuing a doctorate were a caring daughter and a desire to make a difference in other people's lives. I am enjoying the journey and cannot wait until I reach my goal and a new journey begins.

3 My Doctoral Research Journey:
A Controversial Study
Gabriel Flores

I was a struggling doctoral student attending University of Phoenix's educational leadership doctoral program. I started my doctoral journey in May 2004. I was paying for my program in cash and with some student loans. In addition, I was a full-time teacher, teaching 3rd grade students in a Los Angeles suburban school. Oh, and I am a gay Chicano.

Why do I bring up that I am a gay man? Well, I had always heard that to finish a doctoral dissertation, I had better pick a topic about which I am extremely passionate. I was told that if I did not, I would never finish my dissertation and I'd become known as an "ABD" (All But Dissertation). Therefore, I decided that if I am to finish and accomplish my dream of receiving a doctoral degree, I had better pick a topic I was passionate about, and gay issues in education would fit that category.

As a teacher, I loved to teach about tolerance and acceptance during June's "Gay and Lesbian Awareness Month." The Los Angeles Unified School District (LAUSD) strives to have a more inclusive school environment in which all cultures are accepted and mandates June as "Gay and Lesbian Awareness Month." I made it my goal, ever since I began teaching, to include gay culture during multicultural education lessons. Because of this passion, I realized this would make an appropriate dissertation topic.

My first two years as a doctoral student were difficult. I had to get accustomed to the on-line learning format and become even more self-disciplined. Nevertheless, it was a rewarding experience. I had a great cohort, professors, and advisors. During the first two years, I put the scary dissertation behind me. I was not going to worry, just yet. However, I knew it was going to be an arduous journey.

A requirement of the university's doctoral experience is to attend what they referred to as "residencies." All students are required annually to attend a one-to-two-week residency in Phoenix, Arizona. It was a great experience, although at the time it seemed like a nuisance. While there, students took courses, met

22

cohorts personally, and met university staff. Students were provided with nice rooms and all-you-can-eat breakfasts and catered lunches.

The year-two residency was distressing. The topic was finally approaching — the inevitable dissertation. I immediately knew the dissertation is what usually makes or breaks the doctoral student. I had read that 2% of the United States' population has a doctoral degree, and 80% of doctoral students never finish their program. I was shaking in my seat. Nevertheless, I took the dissertation route. I had no choice; I had come this far. I come from a family of scholars. I paid thousands in tuition, and now I owed the government in loans. I could not stop now!

While at the year-two residency, I learned that the first thing I needed to do was start looking for a mentor, dissertation chair, and committee. The university provided the on-line tools, and when I got home, I went at it. I sent e-mails to professors all over the country who might be interested. I knew I was going to get replies because in my e-mail I had my name and an overview of my topic; my topic was extremely controversial, gay-themed literature in the elementary classroom and the attitudes of children. I was very lucky because I acquired a mentor and two committee members almost immediately, to my surprise. My mentor and committee said they were up for the challenge and were quite excited, as I was.

Once I had a mentor, the e-mails to each other began. We e-mailed weekly. My original plan was to study children's attitudes about implementing gay-themed literature in the classroom. I thought that would be an amazing study, as I had been doing that in my classroom for years. Unfortunately, my mentor dissuaded me and said that studying children is risky and usually not approved by the IRB. That was my first unfortunate encounter. I felt sick and sad. What was I then to study?

I remember lying in bed feeling sad and defeated. However, I was not going to stop now, and my mentor pushed me even harder to continue. I remember e-mailing my mentor with many questions, and she never answered as she made me think harder to find answers myself. Then, it suddenly came to me: Why not ask teachers in the LAUSD if they are ready or willing to implement gay-themed literature in the classroom? I e-mailed her immediately, and she was delighted that I had come up with a new dissertation plan. She approved my idea, and on to the next step we went.

The next move was to begin creating the dissertation's chapters, which is a long and arduous process. There was constant revising, editing, rewriting, and even crying. Once a chapter of the dissertation was complete, the editor came next, which was another set of constant revising, editing, rewriting, and crying. Editors were expensive, too. It cost more than $ 6,000 dollars by the time the entire dissertation was complete. Nevertheless, an editor is essential for successful completion of your book.

The next step was to get approval from the LAUSD's external research offices to conduct research within LAUSD premises and teachers. I contacted their office and was surprised by the requirements to achieve access. An additional research proposal and an accompanying survey and cover letter were required. I went ahead and created the documents needed. Initially, I was rejected, and again I felt defeated. However, I eventually took the office's advice and implemented all of their recommendation. After a few weeks of waiting in agony, I finally got the district's approval to conduct my research.

It was time to submit my dissertation proposal to University of Phoenix's ARB (Academic Review Board) and IRB (Institutional Review Board) offices, a full year and a half after beginning the dissertation journey. The Academic Review Board's job was to ensure the study is viable, sound research. The Institutional Review Board's job was to ensure that the research project would not harm any human participants. I was lucky. To my surprise, after three weeks of review, both offices approved the study, and I began the process of data collection immediately thereafter.

The time was June 2008, four years after beginning my doctoral journey. Nine LAUSD Local District 1 schools were chosen to participate in my study. I began the dissemination of surveys and cover letters to teacher participants. That was 300 cover letters and invites to the on-line survey link. I wondered if teachers would even want to participate. June passed by, July passed by, and August passed by. I would look at my on-line data collection tool and realized that only 12 teacher participants had completed the survey. I thought people were not participating for two reasons: Either the topic was too controversial, or people were apathetic to answering surveys, or both. By the time September arrived, I was

26

quite disappointed that there were simply not enough surveys. I understood the study was controversial, and I understood surveys were cumbersome. Nonetheless, my mentor advised I had to conduct a second dissemination.

Mid-September arrived. I had a new 3rd grade class of students, and I had to conduct a completely new dissemination process. Stress was reverberating through my veins. That meant 300 more reminders and 9 more school trips. I was stuffing envelopes and eventually, over a 2-3 day period, I got the surveys disseminated. I had no spit for days. Surveys were in teachers' boxes, and the long wait began again.

One afternoon, I received a phone call from the local District 1 Superintendent's secretary. I was asked who, what, when, and where questions about my survey. Although I had gotten all of the appropriate authorizations from the External Research Office, ARB, and IRB, the superintendent had questions. I had a knot in my stomach; something did not feel right.

Allegedly, a school administrator of one of the participating schools was not happy with surveys being disseminated and had questions about my research study. The administrator contacted her superintendent and complained. That is the reason I got the call from the offices of the superintendent. She wanted a purpose for the research and all accompanying approvals from all of the aforementioned offices. However, even with all of the approvals and an explanation, the superintendent decided to halt all data collection for my study.

I got a call from the same secretary and was no longer allowed to gather data within District 1 schools. I called the office of external research to complain; however, they said that the superintendent always has the last word. I was in turmoil. I thought this was the end of my research study and my doctoral degree. I went home, cried, and thought this was institutional racism or heterosexism, for that matter. Perhaps homophobia on the part of the district, but I had no proof. According to the secretary, the reason for halting data collection was because surveys take time, and teachers might take the surveys during working hours. The reason sounded ridiculous. I felt the statement-undermined teachers' intelligence, and my cover letter clearly stated that all surveys should be completed during their off time.

I e-mailed my mentor and asked what to do next. She said that I should relax and simply accept the data I had already received and to explain in my chapters 4 and 5 what had happened. I was relieved but also disappointed in my district and superintendent. I thought for a minute that if I had not received any data or less than I could have had, I'd have no study and perhaps have to start again. Although my data collection was cut short, fortunately, I had enough data to conduct a qualitative analysis.

In the next few months, I finished my dissertation. I also finished the oral defense. That was one of the scariest times of my life. I had never been so nervous — almost to the brink of vomiting. Nevertheless, it was an amazing experience in the end. A doctoral student simply has to think that the dissertation is really a book of his or her creation and if anyone knows more about the topic, it is the author. I felt comfort in knowing that.

I finally walked on stage for graduation on July 18, 2009. It was exciting for my family and me. I could see the tears running down my father's eyes. I could hear my sister's voice yelling congratulatory phrases as I walked the stage. I could see my mother's smile from a thousand steps away from the stage. I was a happy graduate, one who had completed a controversial study that would eventually have everlasting benefits to society.

There were a few lessons I learned while studying and conducting my research. I learned that patience is important to being a successful doctoral graduate. I learned that diplomacy skills would take you far in reaching your academic goals. Finally, I learned that constructive criticism from others is fine, if only because it is to make you a better learner.

4 My Doctoral War Story
Amanda Grihm

I earned a bachelor degree in communications from Whiting College in Cleveland, OH, in 1978. At the time, I worked as a human resources efficiency expert for an insurance company. I sought out and received a promotion as project communications specialist, which called for attending higher-level meetings and a higher-level of writing skills. At those meetings, I provided overviews of problems with workflow, staffing, and interpreting corporate directives for employees. In essence, I was required to develop communication pieces that translated company goals and objectives in such a manner that it motivated employees to embrace, act upon, and improve their productivity and work ethics.

It did not take me very long to realize that I was in over my head and that my education was inadequate. There were concepts that everyone else seemed to grasp that left me wondering what was going on. Some conversations were so completely out of reach that I could have been an alien observer. I had to ask more questions than I was comfortable asking in order to ensure that I took the appropriate actions. In addition, I worried over what others may have felt about my performance. I began operating from a base of fear. It was not until years later that I realized the concepts comprised industry terms and acronyms that only someone in the business would have known and that many of the concepts were homegrown remedies for the company. My level of discomfort sent me on a covert mission to improve my skills and become an expert at that particular job and just about every other job I've held since that time. My covert activities included devouring subject matter-related materials, getting involved in as many meetings as possible, attending seminars and workshops, taking classes, and soliciting mentors. To others, it appeared I was detailed oriented, autonomous, capable, and a high performer. Realizing that my education was poor caused me to be self-conscious and fearful to the point of feeling paranoid that no matter what I did, my 'lack' would show through all of the polish I had piled on since graduating from Whiting.

Because of my fear of inadequacy, I became proactive on just about everything. I became a critical and analytical thinker—not out of a deep desire for improvement, but out of a deep need to hide the imperfection of an inferior education. I worked at three other places in Cleveland, two government and one corporate, before moving to Atlanta, GA. My insecurity had not diminished, but the jobs I was qualified for and sought became more demanding and important in scope and responsibility. Researching subject matter materials, attending seminars, workshops, and meetings, and seeking mentors had become a part of my normal routine.

The people I worked with had confidence in me. When dubious or doubtful information surfaced, I became the go-to person to validate or invalidate the information. Managers spoke publicly about my ability to find the underlying cause of things, to understand complex issues and break them into bite-sized, manageable pieces of information to help determine the next steps. They described my work and me as "polished," "stimulating," "insightful," "panache," "confident," "knowledgeable," and "educated." I wanted to believe them, and at times, I felt comfortable with, and good about, the results I produced.

When I moved to Georgia in the late 1980s, personal computers were replacing workstations. Software that utilized graphical interfaces like Microsoft Office and IBM Lotus Suites allowed nontechnical people to create, navigate, collaborate, and share documents across secured networks. I understood that technology was on the precipice of redefining work and life, as I knew it. This technology innovation caused the field of information technology to open up to a broader set of skill sets. It was no longer necessary for an engineer to attend MIT or Georgia Tech in order to work in technical fields. This meant that detail-oriented individuals who could follow instructions or processes and procedures, and who could guide customers through scripted technical fixes could secure high-paying technical jobs. It also meant that process-oriented people with good documentation, technical writing skills, and training abilities could easily move into an even higher paying field of information technology. They could frame the areas of responsibility, write the processes and procedures, and train those technicians. That was me! I was detail-oriented, a good communicator who was familiar with process documentation (technical writing), and I had provided training for individuals and corporate and government leaders in previous jobs.

On my second day in Atlanta, I got a job as a temporary employee with IBM. Within the year, IBM/ROLM hired me to work as an IBM/ROLM marketing representative. During my stint as a marketing representative, I took the extra time to correct all of the technical training manuals for my customers. In addition, I developed customer service training for many of my customers and my customers' internal training staffs.

I realized that many of the people I worked and socialized with had master's degrees. They did not appear to be more knowledgeable, committed, or skilled than I was, but their pursuit of an advanced degree gave them greater credence in my own eyes and the advantage in an employer's eyes. In one instance, a co-worker and I applied for the same job. Her master's degree gave her the advantage, and less than a year later, I ended up working for her. She was a smart person and a goal-oriented, smart worker. I watched as she learned her way through the job and used the resources available to help her cement her knowledge on the job. I felt that she was not any smarter or more competent than I was. At that point, I realized that even though I was respected for my work ethic and general knowledge, I was not selected because I had not committed to a higher-level of competence through higher education. I never stopped researching subject matter materials that related to my job, the industry, and leadership. My friends were moving into higher management positions and constantly brainstorming with me on strategic projects. It was those strategy sessions that made me realize that I was as competent and intelligent as the friends who were promoted beyond my reach. Some encouraged me to pursue a master's degree.

In 1986, I witnessed a woman feeding garbage to her baby. That night, I watched the news glibly report on the murder of an 82-year-old woman. My life and my focus changed in an instant. I researched the problems of homelessness for six years, and I volunteered in nursing homes for senior and disabled citizens, part of that time. In 1992, I felt that I understood the problems of homelessness and the plight of seniors who live alone well enough to do something about it. I incorporated and ran a nonprofit 501c3 corporation, Project Match, which matched homeless individuals and single families with senior and disabled citizens who lived alone. I ran Project Match for 13 years on weekends and made more than 200 successful long-term matches. By 2005, the costs had become prohibitive, we found ourselves spending too much on unqualified candidates so the Board and I decided to dissolve Project Match. I decided to get the education that I longed for so that I could put myself in a position to assess and solve long-standing problems like homelessness and the plight of lonely senior and disabled citizens who live alone.

I felt compelled to get a graduate degree. My pursuit to enroll in a master's degree program confirmed my worst fear: My undergraduate degree from Whiting College had not provided me with the education or credentials I needed to get and stay ahead. In fact, when I tried to secure my transcript, I found out Whiting had closed and lost its accreditation before it closed. I was determined to get a credible undergraduate and master's degree. In addition, to make up for the "lack" that I felt for so many years, I also decided to get a doctoral degree.

I could not afford, and did not want, to quit working so I searched for accredited on-line degree programs that offered flexibility and rigor in curriculum. The University of Phoenix seemed to fit my criteria. It was accredited and offers an education enhanced by the world experiences of business people and holders of a host of doctoral and master's degrees. These individuals were learned as well as experienced. To date, I have earned a bachelor of science in marketing and a master of business administration in human resources management. I will complete a doctor of education in educational technology in 2012 from the University of Phoenix. I earned these degrees from the University of Phoenix while working in various demanding roles in corporations and as the founder, chairman of the board, and executive director of Project Match, Inc. Earning these degrees meant 15 to 18 hour days, giving up social activities that were once integral to who I am. It meant bypassing trips for family gatherings, and in 2010, sneaking out in the wee hours of the night to the computer room to get my homework done, while staying at the hospice a few weeks as my younger brother lay dying. In other cases, it meant being taken off the lists of invitees for events hosted by good friends who tired of hearing "Sorry, I can't...." Unbelievably, in some cases, it resulted in lost friendships. In other instances, it resulted in new cohort communities where I share resources and can dialogue about things we care about for hours on end.

My doctoral journey helped me embrace a paradigm shift. I

understand the benefit of knowing that what you do not know may lead to understanding and, further, to new knowledge for my field. I welcome an opportunity to research, learn, simulate, and integrate new knowledge into my life until it becomes meaningful for others and me. My doctoral journey has led me on a journey to find a link between digital technology and the ability to mitigate the explanatory styles and attributions of failure for learned helpless individuals. Learned helpless individuals are those who face so many failures in their lives that they just stop trying to succeed. The dilemma of the learned helpless individual challenges me, and I am committed to finding a solution that will help learned helpless individuals reconnect with and pursue their dreams!

5 Fears and Inhibitions When I Started My Doctoral Journey
Carla Hill

I started my journey by clicking on an ad on Facebook asking what I was planning to do with my mathematics degree. I filled out a questionnaire about my job and interests only to receive back information about on-line schools and programs. I submitted my information to two schools and forgot about it. While on vacation, I received calls from the two colleges. After speaking with the admissions representative from each school and looking at their programs on-line, I decided University of Phoenix had a program in which I was interested. Then the fear and trepidation set in.

I posted on Facebook asking my family and friends if I was crazy to consider returning to school for my doctoral degree at the age of 59. I received overwhelming encouragement from everyone, including my adult daughter. The show of support from those who know me now or knew me in high school was encouraging, and I accepted the journey.

My fears and trepidations only increased once I'd made my decision. I received my master's degree in 1979. I wrote my last research paper in 1973. All I had done for 32 years was teach college students both on-ground and on-line. What made me think I could go back to school for a doctoral degree? Not any school, but an on-line school? I was used to brick-and-mortar schools, including the one in which I teach. I hadn't been a student in 32 years. What made me think that I could still be a successful student? I know from the professor's side that returning students are driven and strive for perfection. With my jobs and other commitments, how could I obtain perfection and find the time to work to the best of my ability?

Before starting the program, my enrollment counselor suggested I take a couple of workshops to get used to the on-line format and to prepare me for the courses I would later take. I chose to take a workshop on APA formatting, since the last paper I wrote was on a typewriter using footnotes. The first night of the APA workshop, my computer crashed! I had looked at the materials before it started and had opened the first work we were to do without a problem. Now it was the course, and I was doing the work. I tried to open the document we were to use and that was it. I had no computer. I had to post the work by 11:59 MST, and I could not submit the work because I had no computer. Panic set in, and I started thinking that here I am taking my first workshop and my first assignment is going to be late. What a way to start my doctoral career!

The next morning, when I arrived at work, I quickly sent an e-mail to the facilitator explaining the situation. I told her that I felt like one of my students making an excuse for not having the work completed! Since it was a workshop, the work wasn't due until the last day so that made me feel better, but I was still frustrated that I now had no computer at home. My work laptop had to travel home with me every night so I could do the work. This was the story for three months before I bought a new laptop for home.

The first course was a writing course. It was designed to see if I was capable of taking the facilitator's feedback and incorporating it in the next version of the paper. The other reason for the course was to see if I could write scholarly. The fears started again as writing was never my forte in high school and college. Luckily, the course was over the summer, so my schedule was a little slower and I had more time. This was the make it or break it course. If I did not pass with a B or better, I was out of the program. As soon as the course was over, I haunted the classroom checking to see if grades were posted so I could take the next course, which started the next day. I passed and continued in the program.

So much of the information in my program is based on K-12 students, and I teach college students. This makes it difficult for me as half the time I don't know what is going on! I do find it interesting because I now know the requirements my students had to meet before they came to college. At times I still feel like I am in over my head. I keep plugging away and trying to do my best and am rewarded with the grades I receive. Eighteen months later, I still wonder what I am doing and what made me think I could do this.

There are high points. When my year-one residency facilitator looked at me and told me I have the knowledge to be a PhD, and that I was just lacking the piece of paper, I thought, maybe I can do this. When my year-two residency facilitator asked me to work with another student to help him sort out his problem statement, purpose statement, and start his proposal, I thought, maybe I am doing the right thing.

44

In a colloquium, I reconnected with the facilitator I had for the make-it-or-break-it composition course. When I mentioned that she was my facilitator for that class, she praised my writing skills and abilities. I was amazed she remembered me and floored to receive such praise for something I always thought was a weakness. I thought, maybe I can do this. Many of my facilitator's praise my writing skills, and I often wish my high school English teacher were still alive to hear what and how I am doing. She would be so pleased! What I always considered a weakness is now seen as strength. Maybe I am not crazy after all. Maybe I can do this.

I am still in awe that I am doing so well. Everything is falling into place. Before year-two residency, I had confirmation from a mentor and both committee members while many of my classmates were still searching. My present facilitator even told me that if I did not have my entire committee, she would love to work with me. This just amazes me that not only do I have my entire committee; I have extras! I guess this is meant to be and I am doing the right thing, even though it is so late in life. I can do this.

6 Gaining My Personal Conviction
Trina Moskalik

I chose to pursue my doctor of management in organizational leadership because I am mentally imbalanced. That must be true. Every person I ever told I was pursuing a doctoral program while working full-time and married with a young child said, "You must be crazy!" After having my application rejected for admission three times due to lack of personal conviction in my future as a doctor, I was ready to walk away. An extra-superfluous degree just to add some initials to my nameplate? It hardly seemed worth all of this, and this was just the application! Facing the personal challenge of overcoming the rejection (a new experience for me) and with some insights from my family, I better understood myself as a learner and a person.

My decision to enroll, and stay, in my doctoral program is a long and arduous one full of APA formatting, long nights, back aches, self-awareness, paper revisions by the truckload, personal growth, and new understandings of the business world. There were nights when my brain literally hurt and my eyes were gritty, and days when I would dance around the computer showing off my very well deserved grades to anyone unfortunate enough to be near me. I can honestly say nothing has been harder (and I am a mom!), and nothing has changed my perceptions of the world more than my doctoral journey. I hope to share my journey with you of starting the program, making it through the first year of courses, and moving into the world of mentors, dissertations, and literature reviews. If nothing else, it should be an amusing tale of a crazy girl and her love of all things personal growth-related.

My doctoral journey started as a whim of a thought: "With some research, it will prove impossible," was my thought. I had wanted to be a medical doctor when I was younger and made my friends call me Dr. Trina for a bit. As I grew up, I realized the dream of becoming a M.D. was not what I thought (easy? glamorous?) and changed tracks to psychology. I thought a psychologist could still help people but would not have to attend medical school and residency programs. After my undergraduate degree, I took the proverbial "year off" before starting my master's program only to lose a decade to work, starting a family, and just living life.

I chose to go back for my MBA because I thought it would help my career, and it did. But, I hated it. The coursework was dry and boring, the topics were all about numbers, and people were forced into the term *human capital*. An MBA is great for many reasons, but I thought so much potential was encompassed in *human capital* and not covered in my program. I knew if I went back to school, it would be to look at the human side of business such as leadership, succession planning, and talent management through organizational effectiveness and development. Competitors can copy a product or a process, but the employees can make a company more or less successful, was my thought.

With six months left in my master's, I started looking at other master's degrees in management or human resources. Then that whim from above kicked in, and I looked at doctoral programs. I actually thought, "How much harder could it be?" from my master's. As I researched more on a doctoral program, it seemed plausible for me to pursue. The possibility of acquiring a doctorate while still working and meeting my social and family obligations was very exciting.

I applied and wrote my essay on why I wanted to earn a doctor of management in organizational leadership. I got rejected due to my lack of conviction about my future as a doctor. Why do I want to be a doctor? "Because it would be cool," was not profound enough for the enrollment department. I was told with such a superficial goal, I would drop out when I hit rigorous courses, and to dig deep and find my true motivation for embarking on this journey. I thought that was my motivation, these people do not even know me, how do they know I would drop out, I don't quit things I start.

I also do not like being told *no*, so I tried again, quoting Walt Disney's "Keep Moving Forward" as a natural academic progression after my master's degree. Denied. So people have to call me Dr. Trina? Nope. So, I asked why other people want to earn their doctorate, but the enrollment representative would not tell me that. Geez, this may have been a bad idea after all, what are they looking for in terms of motivation from me? I put it aside and thought it was not worth it and I would just get another master's degree after all. But I could not let the idea go about being a doctor.

50

So, I wrote another essay. I wrote about my passionate belief that education is the one thing that cannot be taken from you, and if we are not learning we are wasting time. I also mentioned how I thought my then 4-year-old daughter would feel when at age 7 or 8 she could watch me walk across the stage for that honor of becoming a doctor. I wrote about how great it would be to help the next generation of learners as a faculty member at another college. I also mentioned that I wanted the accomplishment so my family, friends, *and I* can be proud of me: This is an arduous journey that few start and even fewer finish. I was accepted to the program.

I did not mention any practitioner ideas, as I had none at the time, and over the last two and a half years, that has given me the most reward for my schooling. I cannot wait to bring all of my ideas to my employer and show how we can benefit from these ideas and the natural fit for some theoretical models into our organization. I think the true beauty of a doctoral degree is the ideas we can help create, expand, and use in our organizations and for future academia.

After the celebratory dance around my house came the finer points of the acceptance letter. I had to take a three-week, pass-orfail workshop to get fully accepted. The letter was for probationary approval, conditional on my passing this course. I had just finished my master's degree so I was not worried about a communications course to test my formatting and proficiency levels. I should have been. The words "academic rigor" were introduced to me in this course. I used 'most,' 'many,' 'lots,' 'few,' and other vague words in my writing that were not academic enough for doctoral work. "Past tense only." "No first person." "Passive voice violations." If I can't use first person, and passive voice is not allowed, how do I make a sentence? "Anthropomorphisms?"—I had to Google that one. I had never seen so much red on a paper of mine before, and then the sources page…YIKES! I started to worry that the stupid entrance essay had been the easy part of this whole journey (it was), and wondering what had I gotten myself into now. I passed the workshop by only half a point.

I called my college counselor and suggested maybe I should stop and not go into the program. If I could barely pass the workshop, how was I ever going to make the grade in the program or write a 200+ page dissertation? We spoke for about ten minutes, and she basically told me it was my decision to stay or not, and the workshop was supposed to be hard. The course typically weeds out 20% of potential students who were not committed. I had 48 hours to decide, or I would be enrolled in my first course and committed financially.

I did what any self-respecting, married, 30-year-old professional woman and mother would do: I called my mom for advice. She is a high school teacher, so she knows the value of education, knows my schedule, and most important, knows me. We spoke for quite a while and talked out both sides of the what-if scenarios objectively. I decided I could not live with the regret of not going for it. If I failed, then at least I tried. She also pointed out that I had never failed at anything I really wanted, so I had to ask *do I really want to earn this degree?* I was in the next class on Tuesday, fully committed to the program.

It was an organizational development and managerial historic perspective course reviewing the history of management in corporations. I was fascinated to learn the theories and how they had grown and changed over the centuries. I was so glad I had decided to stay; these were the topics I wanted to learn about. I got into a routine, learned more about formatting and writing at the doctoral level, and really got into the groove of the program.

Then I hit the philosophy coursework.

For those of you not aware, there are two main types of doctoral degrees: practitioner and philosophical. The philosophical one is the PhD most think of when someone is getting a doctoral degree; it covers the theories in a field of study. A practitioner degree is for people who are applying what they are learning to a field of study—such as a doctor of medicine is a practitioner degree, or one who practices. I chose a practitioner degree because what use is the theory if I do not know how to apply it in the real world, was my thought process. I would not go to a doctor that knew the history of pneumonia but not how to cure it. I did not think I would like philosophy, as it seemed to be talking in circles with no right answer. I was right. It is horrible. It was circular and confusing; I had read and reread passages from the texts. I had to read it aloud. I had to phone a friend and read it to her. I had no idea what the questions or assignments meant to find an answer to them. I felt frustrated and stupid- I was not alone in these feelings. My classmates were struggling along beside me through Nietzsche, deconstruction theory, and post-modernism. As I wrote my papers, I had no idea what I was talking about. It felt like the more I babbled and rambled, the better the grade I got. The purpose of the courses was to teach us to look at problems differently, think in new ways, and understand large themes of great scholars. What did I get out of it? I got a B+, and the strong desire never to step foot into a philosophy class ever again—and maybe some of that other stuff, too.

Those 18 weeks of frustration, fear, and feeling like a failure were as close as I got to dropping out of the program. I relied on everyone in my class to vent to, my mom and husband to cheer me on, and my work to distract me from it. This is the key to success at the doctoral level. Having passion for your topic of study and a strong network of people to support you when it gets tough will get you through the program. And so it went for another year and a half of courses. Work really hard through a course, complain to classmates about the amount of work we have, and then relax for a week. The week off between courses always seemed too short, and most of the time I was already looking at the next course. Every A felt like an accomplishment so large it should have been made public, every B was an embarrassment to my support system. In the end the grades are the least important part of the process; the information I now have in my head, the self-awareness I have gained as I learned about leadership and management styles, and the ideas I have for my future are what I actually earned from each course.

I started my dissertation last week on Valentine's Day of 2012; I have a few courses left. I know this is a critical time in my program as a large portion of doctoral students go ABD (all but dissertation) and never finish their program. I have a class/work schedule that I am used to, and I am adhering to it for my dissertation now. The two hours I used to spend on homework I now spend on writing and research to submit my proposal for institutional approval to begin my research. The end is in sight, but the road is steep to get there. I am intimidated and excited by the idea of a dissertation, but I cannot wait to see the finished product sometime in 2013. Even better is the idea of getting my title of Dr. Trina. Finally, I may require everyone I know to call me that for a few weeks as a tribute to my efforts. In reality, I will probably just take a much needed, well deserved, long vacation to somewhere with no Internet access and not bring my computer. That actually sounds a bit like heaven, but not before I finish the program. One more year of grinding out my education, then who knows what the possibilities may be for me, but I will know that nothing I can ever attempt again in the future can be more intense and rewarding at the same time.

7 Keeping the Faith: A Doctoral Journey
Karen F. Phillips

Why did I undertake a doctoral program at this point in my life? Completing a doctoral program is an arduous undertaking in the best of circumstances. In addition, the program I enrolled in was on-line. Most of my friends thought I was crazy to consider something of this nature at my age. But my family and those who knew me well were aware of my continued thirst for knowledge and my love of learning. I was often referred to as a perpetual student. There were those who told me I was kidding myself to think I would be able to complete the program. Their negativity probably made me even more determined to succeed; that and the fact that I always wanted to be a doctor. Some even told me they thought it was selfish of me to enroll in a doctoral program particularly as I had children nearing college age. Interestingly enough, next to my husband, my children were my biggest supporters. They often told their friends that their mother was going to be a doctor. At the doctor's office where I worked for 16 years, many of the patients referred to me as Dr. Karen. I always thought that had a good ring to it and knew that one day I would achieve that coveted title. Obtaining my doctoral degree was always my dream, but I knew achieving this milestone would not be without its challenges.

And so I began taking the steps to make my dream a reality. I spoke with an admissions counselor at University of Phoenix (UOP) on-line. Then I had a telephone interview with both the admissions counselor and the director of doctoral admissions. Financial aid was squared away, my books were ordered, and I was ready to begin. The first course of the doctoral program was considered a weeding-out course. Students received only a provisional acceptance into the doctoral program until the first course was completed satisfactorily. I remember feeling so much anxiety through that first course as I sought to prove I belonged in this program. The course was only three weeks long, so I had to manage the time allotment for assignments and participation very carefully. Daily chats with my admissions counselor went a long way toward allaying my anxiety as he offered much encouragement and support. Unfortunately, he left UOP two weeks into that first course, but the doctoral admissions manager continued to counsel me through the remainder of that all-important first course. When the final grade was posted, I received an A and had earned my spot in the doctoral program. I was so relieved. My doctoral journey now officially had begun.

Although I chose an EdD over a PhD, working toward an EdD was more challenging for me because I didn't have much of an education background. In my master's program, I had only one or two education courses related to curriculum. I felt this was a true limitation for me, and this was the primary reason I decided to pursue an EdD. I knew I lacked the necessary educational components that would make me a better educator. With 30 years of nursing experience, I felt comfortable with my nursing knowledge and skills. I had very little knowledge of or experience with classroom management or instructional strategies. Another reason I decided upon an EdD was that I perceived a PhD to be more research-oriented and less people-oriented. Being a nurse, I am more of a people person. Skills like communication and active listening are essential components of my everyday life as a nurse and educator. These were skills I did not want to lose.

Another barrier I faced was my limited technology skills. I barely used e-mail and didn't know much about PowerPoint or Word. My husband, Ken, set up my laptop so I could go right to the UOP icon and connect to my classroom. My children (Marc, Cara, and Ryan) helped me a little with PowerPoint, but I pretty much taught myself Word by trial-and-error. I felt there were probably time-saving techniques, but I didn't have time to take a course, even a basic one, so I had to make do with what I knew. To say APA format, grammar, Word, and even my typing skills were weak was a gross understatement. However, I persevered, and my skills improved thanks in large part to the writing center and feedback from members of my cohort. I also should add that having UOP tech support available 24/7 was lifesaving, as most of my technology issues always happened after everyone else in my house was already asleep. Tech support was definitely a strong point for UOP; the support staff always remained on the line until the problem was solved. In my case, that was sometimes an hour or more. I will be eternally grateful to the countless individuals in tech support who assisted me with such patience and perseverance.

Being a student myself really enabled me to relate better to what my students were going through in trying to balance their lives, work, school, and families. I was able to offer them suggestions for strategies that had worked for me and, whenever possible, tried to clarify assignments. I always disliked that aspect of my doctoral program when I would ask questions of my facilitators and they would rephrase the question for me, never actually clarifying what I didn't understand. Another pet peeve of mine was that we had to go into a detailed explanation to tell them what we had done already to find the answers, and still very few facilitators were really helpful. Sometimes I spent many hours researching and coming up empty, which was very frustrating. I literally had no more time to look. I didn't expect them to give me the answers; all I wanted was a little direction.

APA format was another challenge for me. Facilitators seemed to have their own version of APA and not necessarily the one approved by the American Psychological Association. Each time I got feedback, I made changes as suggested by the course facilitator. Each time I started a new course, the new facilitator would mark it wrong, so I would correct it again. The inconsistencies from facilitator to facilitator continued throughout most of the program. It wasn't until the last year of my program that my facilitators were in agreement on APA format. Then as I finally completed my dissertation, the change was made to APA 6th edition. At that point, I felt I needed an editor in order to ensure I had the correct format to get my dissertation approved by the dean. That was an expensive proposition, one you don't really know about until you are well into the process. Although I believe the money was well spent, having an idea of that expense earlier in the process would have been helpful.

The mentor-mentee connection was another source of stress; we had to select a mentor and committee members from an approved list of primarily unknown persons. For many of my colleagues and me, the process involved blindly selecting individuals we hoped would meet our individual needs based solely on their biographies. As it happened, several potential mentors I e-mailed never responded to my request. I felt it was so unprofessional to not even respond at all. Luckily for me, one of my facilitators at year-two residency recommended a mentor, and another facilitator I had met face-to-face agreed to be on my committee. Having found my mentor and one committee member decreased my stress level a great deal. My mentor gave suggestions for my final committee member. With that important issue resolved, I felt more comfortable with the process at that point. Every class I was in, all my facilitators kept telling me how lucky I was to have the mentor I had. Having that kind of feedback made me feel much better about my selection.

Even with all the support I had, I found trying to balance work, family, and school to be extremely stressful. Time management was crucial to maintain any type of balance. Since I generally have many irons in the fire at once, I thought time management would not be problematic for me. I always have been active in my community, but I soon realized I would have to curtail some of my volunteer activities in order to keep up with the workload from my doctoral courses and maintain some semblance of family life. Additionally, I tried various stress management strategies such as music, walking, and breathing techniques in an effort to reduce the overwhelming stress I felt. There were many times I questioned my decision to enroll in a doctoral program. I had very little free time, and my family shouldered the brunt of the household chores. I rarely had time for my friends or family, and the yearly required residencies were extremely stressful.

Halfway through my second year in the program, I started my first course with my mentor. Then I received the diagnosis that no one wants to hear: I had breast cancer. I couldn't even say the words *breast cancer* let alone comprehend what was ahead for me. When I received the news, I had just written a rough draft of Chapter 1 and had not even started Chapter 2 of my proposal. During that class, I underwent two separate surgeries two weeks apart. After the lumpectomy and node dissection, I found it difficult to lift my arm let alone write and type because the surgery was on my right side and I am right handed. I was in a lot of pain, but focusing on my writing helped distract me as I waited for answers.

That was only the beginning of my journey into the unknown. I was still reeling from the unexpected news of the breast cancer. I met with my surgeon to get the final pathology report and hardly remembered much of what he said. Luckily, my husband was there with me, and he remembered everything we had to do. Afterwards, I had to meet with both medical and radiation oncologists to get their opinions to determine my next course of treatment. Prior to starting any treatments, I had numerous tests to ensure the cancer had not spread. I was informed I needed chemotherapy as well as radiation. It was at this time that I remembered my mantra during my master's program: *"Keep the faith."* That mantra kept me going during challenging times in my master's program, and I hoped it would do so now. I put my faith in God and in myself. For the next six months, every three weeks, I went to get blood work and see the oncologist. If all my counts were normal, I would get the chemotherapy treatment. Each time I spent the entire afternoon at the oncologist's office, as it took roughly three hours for the treatment.

Throughout the treatment regime, I not only had the coursework to complete, but also had to make revisions to chapters one and two of my proposal. I thought about applying for a leave of absence, but all my doctors advised against that. They all thought continuing my coursework and working on my proposal would help distract me from worrying about the diagnosis of cancer and how it would impact my life. When it was time for my treatments, I always brought my books and reading materials so I could work on my assignments for UOP and stay on schedule with my courses and writing my proposal. Keeping the faith allowed me to stay focused on my goal and kept my journey on track. I felt God was with me every step of that journey, enabling me to find the strength to move forward in spite of the challenges I faced.

My medical oncologist would always reinforce how important she thought it was for me to keep going with my doctoral studies. Both she and my surgeon wrote letters to allow me to get accommodations from the Office of Disability so I could get extra time for my assignments. This helped a lot. Then if I was having a particularly bad week after chemotherapy, I could delay working on the assignments until I felt better. Luckily, most of the side effects of the chemotherapy treatments were well managed with the medications they gave me. I was really tired the first few days after the treatments, sometimes too tired or nauseous to read or research for assignments. Often I had to rest in the afternoon, particularly because I still had my position as a clinical nursing instructor, which was exhausting in conjunction with the chemotherapy and radiation.

After a particularly difficult round of chemotherapy, I had to leave within a week to go to Arlington, Virginia, for my third and hopefully final residency. This residency was 8 days in length and was expected to last at least 8-9 hours a day. Up to this point, I had barely managed to work 4-5 hours a day and then I had to rest. I really didn't know how I would manage at residency where I had to stay in the classroom so long. I was really worried. Two weeks before I was to leave, my white count was low and I had to get an injection of Neulasta, a medication used to raise my white blood cell count. The Neulasta worked, and my white count went up to normal. Unfortunately, one of the side effects of this medication was bone pain that was unrelieved by anything but strong pain relievers that made me even more tired. I could hardly move without the painkillers, as the pain was so intense. Trying to focus on assignments prior to residency was particularly difficult because of all the side effects I was experiencing from the chemotherapy and the Neulasta. I really didn't know until the week before residency if I could get medical clearance to go. I was so relieved when my oncologist said it was okay.

Even with the permission of my oncologist, I still wasn't sure I would get through those long days and evenings that were typical of the UOP residencies. We usually had team assignments or presentations or both to complete for the next day's class; we had to work on them after class was finished each day. Once again, I relied on my faith to help me get through those long days. A plus of being at residency was being around the members of my cohort and the network of colleagues I developed during my doctoral journey. They could attest to how physically and mentally draining residency was without the additional stress of the cancer treatments. Many individuals were solicitous of my health and well being during that time. I'll never forget their concern and how much that meant to me. When we started this program, we were all relative strangers. Each year we would meet at residency and catch up on the events of our lives over the past year. Each residency was a mini reunion. Even knowing the work that lay ahead, I looked forward to residency and seeing all my colleagues once again.

The last year after the coursework was completed was the most difficult primarily because of the isolation I experienced without the support of my cohort group. I think most individuals in the doctoral program at UOP could relate to the loneliness of this time. Trying to get the proposal written and approved without having that group support was challenging at best. I was working one-on-one with my mentors and committee members, but it wasn't the same as having that group support from my cohort. Along with this, I had to start my radiation treatments and was experiencing tremendous fatigue from them. With these treatments, I had to go daily for six weeks. Naps were common during this time because of the exhaustion I was experiencing. But I finally got the proposal approved; the study completed, passed the oral defense, and finished my dissertation. My dissertation was approved the first time it was submitted. I was excited and exhilarated. My mentor told me that only a handful of students received dissertation approval on the first submission. I considered myself lucky to have overcome all the obstacles I faced and completed the program. It was clear to me that keeping the faith had allowed me to succeed in my doctoral program.

Through my doctoral journey, I also developed some lifelong friendships. Two very close friends from my cohort, Rose B. and Tammy M., were the glue that helped me keep it together during residency, through the coursework, and during the dissertation process. Along with my family, they were with me every step of the way from the beginning when I was diagnosed with breast cancer. I couldn't have continued on in this rigorous program without their unrelenting support. This was particularly true during the process of developing and getting the proposal approved, conducting the study, and writing the dissertation. We were constantly in touch via e-mail or phone bouncing ideas off each other and even practicing for the oral defense. They were my lifelines, and my life is so much richer because they are part of it. I don't know anyone in the doctoral program who didn't face obstacles and barriers. But at the end of the journey, I persevered through the program despite my breast cancer treatments and was successful. I also have to acknowledge my colleagues at the university and the nurses I worked with at the hospital for their continued support and encouragement during this time.

Aside from the friendships I developed, attending and participating in graduation in Phoenix was the highlight of my achievement of my doctoral degree. Everyone I met made such a fuss, applauding as we walked into UOP stadium, offering congratulations, and making me feel so special. I finally got to meet my mentor and some of my course facilitators, which was so exciting. Putting on the doctoral robes for the first time was inspiring and hearing my name, Dr. Karen Phillips, was a surreal experience. Marching in amidst all the applause made me feel like I was someone special, someone important. I know I had tears in my eyes when I walked onto that stage and was hooded. Keeping the faith in my abilities and myself allowed me to achieve my goal. My dream was finally a reality. I was finally Dr. Karen, and it was everything I imagined it would be.

8 The "Stuff" They Don't Tell You
Holly Rick

Early in my higher education experience, I was told I was not smart and that I would never amount to anything. My decision to go to an on-line school proved it in some people's eyes: Why would I go to an on-line university to obtain a doctoral degree? I could not really answer why I wanted the degree. I had never really thought it through. I have to be honest and say that I did not know the difference between a doctorate and a PhD, but I wanted an advanced degree at any cost.

With no set goal in mind, finding the right program was difficult. Four months after finishing my MBA degree, I told my boyfriend (who is now my husband) that I was bored. I told him I wanted to go back to school. He was mad that I even wanted to entertain the idea having due dates and more debt. After much discussion and compromise, he helped me create a list of requirements that I decided I needed in a program. I knew that I had a passion for management and leadership. With a few clicks of my mouse, I weighed the pros and cons of numerous schools and made my choice to enroll. I never looked back and never regretted the decision. I am proud of my experience in the classroom and believe to this day that on-line education is difficult. It requires personal drive.

Prior to starting the doctoral program, I was very social. I would go out numerous nights a week, plan outings for my family and friends, and always have people stopping by my home. I loved this life and really believed that I could keep up this busy schedule while working full-time and adding doctoral studies. I was wrong; time management was the one thing I had to do and I had to learn to do it well. When enrolling in the program, I figured I would need to spend at least 15 to 20 hours a week studying. That amount of study time sounded like too much, but I soon found it was the minimum. I did not have time to be the social person that my friends had once known. No one told me I would have to adjust my personal time and make choices about what personal commitments to attend. I struggled through the first few classes in my program. I attended my first residency, where I learned that I was going to have to make a choice. I could keep my social life or make changes so I could complete the degree. I missed birthday parties and celebrations to make sure that I made deadlines and had read the required material. Sometimes I did leave the homework, allowing myself to sneak to a few engagements and celebrations. Even though it was hard to miss out on what I loved, I can look back and know that I made a great decision to allow myself the time to do the doctoral work.

Develop professional relationships was what I was told I would need to do; I personally had a hard time doing that in the on-line classroom. I might not have the same students in the next class, and I found that people did not really want to get to know each other. They were busy like me trying to get the work completed. The last thing on many of the students' minds was developing professional relationships. That is a regret that I have. Back when I was in school, we did not have Facebook or other social media to form support groups and relationships. I have taken action to help in my building of support groups. I have created my presence on social media and at conferences, and while I have not been able to connect with previous peers, I have reached out to former faculty and other professionals that have my same interests. While I feel late in getting my professional relationships, I do feel that I have made strong relationships and look forward to continued cultivation of those relationships.

Truly knowing and understanding the theoretical aspect of the subject I was learning was something I did not grasp at first. I had heard people say I was going to become the expert in what I was going to research, but that did not resonate, either. It was not until I attended a conference with other academics that I understood what they meant. At the first academic conference I attended, I was reserved and sat back to listen. I heard the participants talk about their research and how they were applying theories that were important to them. I wanted to be like them. I studied harder and really learned to apply theories to what was happening in the workplace. Then I had experiences to share with academics, and at my next conference I no longer sat listening. I was part of the conversation.

Being punctual was the hardest lesson I have learned. During my comprehensive and dissertation phase, I got married. Although I was still paying tuition and supposed to be working hard, I wasn't getting all of the work done that I needed to. I missed deadlines, had to re-register for class, and pay additional tuition. I wish that someone had told me to make a plan and set deadlines I was willing to stick to. During the dissertation phase, I stopped communicating with my mentor. I felt he would be disappointed in me because I was not finishing in a timely manner, and I had not reached out to him. Finally, I did contact him. He was very happy that I was fine, and even though I did not make progress, he wanted to continue working with me. It was the reassurance I needed to get over the hump and get started writing again. Learning how to communicate effectively and not be afraid of letting people down would have saved me not only money but also the stress of not making progress.

I always started my goal setting with a huge milestone. When I started the doctorate, my goal was to finish. As I look back about that goal, I must admit that I did it wrong. I made it through my coursework fine; it all went downhill when I started focusing on my comprehensive exam and the dissertation. I let life take over. I changed jobs, planned my wedding, and had a baby. I was not focusing on my work. I was overwhelmed by the amount of work that went into the dissertation. I found that having one big overall goal was not motivating me. I had to make small goals: if I wrote ten pages, I could go and get a pedicure. I had to create realistic goals to ensure that I could meet them.

Creating good, professional scholarly writings and assignments was something that I thought that I had always done. Being in a doctoral program has shown me what good writing looks like. It's tough when you receive your first paper back and there are more red marks and feedback than I wrote for the paper requirement. Learning how to take the feedback, to look at it as a critical review not a smack down, and incorporate the changes into the next set of assignments was key to my development. The first time I received feedback, I almost quit the program; I felt I had done so poorly that the rest of my program would be too hard and I would not be able to handle it. I applied the feedback and quickly found that my writing improved. As I worked through the classes, I found that I was a good writer, and I could communicate in scholarly terms.

After I graduated, I made up my mind that I wanted to work in higher education. Finding the next step after I graduated was not easy. There is a stigma among many folks about on-line doctoral programs. On-line education is like any other program. You get good faculty and bad faculty. You get faculty who provide you with great feedback, and some who do not provide any feedback. The expectations of an on-line program are the same as a ground program. As a student, you must read, comprehend, and analyze what you are reading. You have to be able to convey your thoughts on topics and research well to support your thoughts. It is harder on-line when you don't have that faculty member in your face asking you about your work. But I love on-line education; I am proud of my position as a campus chair working with doctoral students in an on-line environment.

I will admit that I let life happen while I was in my program. I allowed life and other fun things to happen, putting off due dates and not holding myself accountable. I did not take the time or cultivate the relationships with my peers or others whom I could mentor. I thought that I was a great communicator but found out quickly that I had so much to learn.

I got married, had a baby, and was five months pregnant when I walked across the stage at graduation. I would not change my experience as a doctoral student and now academic. Your doctoral journey is so much more than researching and meeting a goal. It is a journey where you are in the driver's seat; you will hear horror stories of other people's journeys. Keep in mind that these are their journeys. The best advice I can give is that you own your doctoral journey, embrace it, communicate, develop relationships, set your goals, and become the expert that people expect from someone with a doctoral degree. The doctoral journey is only the beginning to a new way of life; own it.

9 Soldiering My Way to the Top
Carl Schwander

The year is 1992; the halls of Union High School in Grand Rapids, Michigan, fill with pupils and teachers eager to meet the many personalities of the year. One of my freshman classes is entitled "Upward Bound," a class designed to expose students to future college opportunities and experiences. Little to my knowledge I would seek a doctoral degree some 20 years later. My involvement with the high school Junior Reserve Officer Training Corps (JROTC) program and the local hospital (Butterworth) VolunTEEN program set the foundation upon which I would continue to serve my country.

My take-away from the Upward Bound class was a phrase said to me by Mr. Hinton, "Remember the world owes you nothing, but will require much of you." It is true — no one is going to hand you a worry-free life, "success in a bag ready to go." The achievement of emotional, physical, and educational wealth must be earned through years of give and take. As a young man growing up, I was happy to receive a quality public education.

This pursuit of a better life — the ability to buy my own things, support a family, and create opportunity — required hard work and personal effort. My enlistment in the United States Army was finalized about 90 days after graduating from high school in 1996. My travels have taken me across continents, time lines, and cultures. Two deployments to Korea, one to Iraq, and four years on the recruiting trail provided endless hours to manage my personal and professional goals. I have persisted in enrolling in college courses while in the U.S. Army, attending classes overseas, and even while in combat in 2003 during Operation Iraqi and Enduring Freedom. After completing my master of public administration degree from the University of Phoenix in 2007, I realized that I still had a taste for expanding my knowledge.

My journey to doctoral status began in January 2008, learning and advancing my critical thinking skills to their maximum capacity. The first thing I remember about doctoral studies was this statement from a professor during orientation, "The reins are off when seeking doctoral work; learners are encouraged to ask questions. Technical experts don't just respond — they create." My first residency in Arlington, Virginia, provided the necessary tools for doctoral communication, research assistance, and team building emphasis. The University of Phoenix doctoral program offers the "Scholar, Practitioner, Leader" model as their recipe for doctoral students to learn, develop, and report professional works. I have found that this model can be replicated in the workplace, interacting with others without bias or preconceived notions.

Doctoral residency is the opportunity for the learner to collaborate with team members, meet faculty and staff, and validate academic achievement. A key benefit of seeking a doctoral degree is the excitement of separating yourself from your peers and pushing personal limits. Doctoral projects include team-based assignments, dissemination of responsibilities, and expanding one's exposure to peer-reviewed resources. My year-two residency offered a number of new perspectives to jump-start personal thought about paradigm creation and dissertation topics. After traveling across the world while stationed in South Korea, I was able to spend my birthday with my girlfriend Katelyn during the year-two residency in Arlington, Virginia. On March 23, 2010, (little did she expect) under the watchtower of a lighthouse on Lake Michigan, I asked for her hand in marriage. One week later I returned to Korea and began my next doctoral class.

My return to Fort Sill, Oklahoma, in August of 2010 provided me with a generous opportunity to seek out my examination audience. Since child-support enforcement laws had been a significant part of my life—two children from a previous marriage—why not interview and examine how child support influences active duty military members at Fort Sill? Year-three residency offers hours of one-on-one time with doctoral coaches, who help the learner, answer his or her topics and questions. Considering a wedding in three months and another residency approaching, the U.S. Army was gracious enough to provide me with 20 days of free leave.

Success comes from countless research hours and numerous personal and professional compromises. The extensive work needed for the completion of a dissertation is not something that can be taken with a grain of salt; this is going to take every bit of your mind and time. Key advice from my year-three residency was, "Don't come back for year four." Individuals who lose themselves along the way are required to attend year-four residencies some two years later for re-examination, assistance, and an opportunity to submit their proposal.

As June 2011 approached, I managed a dissertation completion course and my wedding one thousand miles away in Dayton, Ohio. Our honeymoon consisted of a Brad Paisley concert and dinner at Red Robin in Indianapolis, Indiana. My mentor, Dr. Reece, was nice enough to provide me a week off from class to celebrate and enjoy time with my new wife. My proposal and ideas were constantly evolving, demanding my time, energy, and patience. Perfecting the proposal requires tools, resources, and selecting the right editor.

Selecting an editor can be exhausting but a necessary examination of professional work. My editor provided extensive details on proper citing procedures, word usage, and sentence structure. During a voice and e-mail conversation and exchange of professional references I agreed to her services. After sending her my proposal, she told me the finished product would be ready in four days. Two weeks passed, and no response from the editor, no e-mail or telephone calls — and more important — no edited proposal. A class member told me the editor was in the hospital with kidney failure. I was not sure if I needed to hire a new editor or a lawyer to get my deposit from her estate.

One month later, her apology arrived, saying she'd had personal matters that interfered with her ability to complete the work on time. After ensuring my editor was alive, I was able to proceed with my first edit of chapter's 1-3. Upon receipt of the finished product, I realized I had sent a 20,000-word document instead of a 10,000-word document, a difference of $ 250.00. To this date, my editor has been extremely professional and answers any questions I have along the way. Looking back on my experience, I recommend students use an individual editor instead of one from a large business or mass-editing house. Professional relationships require strong communication and a savvy networking outlook.

Committee member selection can be stressful and confusing. Finding professionals willing to give their time and experience is frustrating when project constraints and conflicts interfere with personal agendas. I have fired two committee members because of either an inability to respond or to make deadlines. A positive contribution in my doctoral journey has been my mentor, Dr.

Amanda Reece. Selecting the right mentor is instrumental in assisting with difficult questions, providing guidance through the dissertation process, and establishing achievable goals.

The creation of scholarly work takes time and patience. Plentiful professional papers, discussion questions, team assignments, and finally the birth of my doctoral proposal brought me to my present endeavor, *"Soldiers' Perceptions of Child Support Enforcement Resources."* Learning how to write effectively, understand proper use of direct quotes, and operate the school resource center are fundamental aspects of knowledge creation. To this point I have completed the remainder of my classes and have yet to conduct my research. The term "All But Dissertation" (ABD) will have to work until I can produce a quality research study.

10 In Pursuit of a Terminal Degree: A Sexagenarian's Doctoral Journey

Mary J. Stedman

Returning to school at any age is a major decision requiring serious thought and planning. The decision I made in 2008 was not easy but one I will never regret. In August 2008, just shy of my 60th birthday, a time when many are considering slowing down and eventual retirement, I was seriously investigating doctoral programs. Was I crazy, or just experiencing a mid-life crisis ten years later than most people? The phrase, *terminal degree*, has taken on a new and more humorous connotation as I near completion of the most challenging and satisfying journey I have ever taken. Perhaps my chosen career of nursing had something to do with my thinking.

As a nurse educator, I frequently have occasion to discuss Erikson's (1963) developmental stages with students and colleagues. My age clearly positions me somewhere between middle adulthood and late adulthood. Furthermore, I found myself immersed in thoughts of generativity versus stagnation or integrity versus despair depending on the time of the day or the situation I was facing (Erikson). On some days, the idea that I could really finish any doctoral program, no less the one I was enrolled in, seemed ridiculous. On other days I was hopeful. I decided on applying to an on-line EdD program with a specialization in curriculum and instruction. Although many thought I needed my head examined, I chose this curriculum because I knew it would enhance my ability to teach my students effectively, and it also might serve as a stepping stone to a new retirement career for me in on-line education. I already have experience teaching courses on-line, which is something I truly enjoy and would like the opportunity to expand.

Qualifying Course "The Test"

One of my greatest fears as I ventured forth was that I would never be able to pass the qualifying course because I never considered myself a good writer. Before long, however, I realized that my writing skills would have little influence on my success or failure. Instead, it would be life's personal and family responsibilities that would present me with some of my greatest challenges. As I began the program, I knew immediately that I would need to become more organized and better able to manage my time. I survived the on-line orientation and began the qualifying course.

As a full-time professor, I found myself traveling to present a conference paper at the same time I was trying to complete my first assignment for school. Surviving the first week, I entered the second week with a renewed sense of confidence — only to have a close relative die suddenly, placing a tremendous amount of pressure on me to complete assignments in less time than I would have preferred. I anticipated the third and final week would be easy compared with the first two. Much to my surprise, however, the third week would present my greatest challenge. With three days left in the course and the clock ticking down, my husband was seriously injured in a truck accident at work and hospitalized in a trauma intensive care unit. Could this be happening? How will I finish the course? Am I meant to complete this program?

The answer was, you bet I am! For some reason, I believe the events of those first few months occurred so that I would know just how much I wanted this degree and just how hard I was going to need to work to complete it. The following essay presents powerful reflections on the challenges faced as I progressed through the next three years. In a series of short vignettes, I share useful information on how to survive and hopefully complete a doctoral program in your 60s. Topics included are how to surround oneself with effective support systems and creatively and effectively manage your time even when you need to work full-time. How does age affect one's choices and what effect does age have on the outcomes? Personal and professional challenges I faced are presented in a manner that is both serious and humorous at the same time.

"The Green S and the Red U"

Once I successfully completed the qualifying course, I immersed myself in the first official curriculum course on leadership. The content seemed manageable, and the faculty member, approachable. The next ten weeks actually provided some of the most intense moments, as well as some of the most humorous that I have endured. As the course unfolded, I was introduced to an evaluative process involving the use of a Green S depicting a satisfactory response and a Red U that stood for unsatisfactory.

Perhaps, I forgot to mention this earlier, but the program I am enrolled in is an on-line program that includes three in-person residencies over the course of the program. Well, the Green S and the Red U almost proved to be my undoing. Although I never considered myself to be a Type A personality or even obsessive compulsive, my desire to do well academically began to affect my every move.

The on-line environment can be tricky. Not everything is as crystal clear as the case of the Green S and the Red U. Having taught on-line myself for almost ten years, I really thought I understood the process and proceeded to participate in the on-line classroom. Much to my horror, I became aware that not only was I receiving Green S's for my participation posts, I also was receiving Red U's. I can honestly share that I don't think I had seen that much red ink since grammar school, and I was horrified and at the same time humiliated even though I was the only one who could see them. Fearing the worst, that I would need to withdraw and abandon my quest for the EdD, I decided to swallow hard and e-mail the professor to ask what was wrong with my submissions. Much to my surprise and delight, there was nothing wrong with my submissions at all. What I didn't realize is that even though the Green S signaled an acceptable participation post, the Red U only signaled that the submission did not count toward participation but rather was a course requirement. The moral of this story is to think before you leap to conclusions, and ask questions, lots of questions.

"Hot Air"

The next critical hurdle would be surviving residency. One of the best decisions I ever made was to attend a residency close enough to home to allow driving there and to travel with my close friend and colleague, who started the same program approximately three weeks after I did. With a little help from admissions and academic advisors, we were able to schedule and attend residency together. Having a friend with whom to share this experience was perhaps one of the most significant factors contributing to my success. The fact that she, too, is a sexagenarian is priceless. As the residency unfolded, the two of us knew instinctively that we would need each other and all of the stamina in the world to make it to the finish line. As the first day began, we were assigned to different classrooms, which didn't make either of us happy, but there was nothing we could do about it. We each went our way, knowing that we would meet up again at dinner and be able to share the highs and lows of the day.

What I don't think either of us expected was the grueling nature of the all-day class followed by evening team meetings and finishing touches on assignments and course papers. Were all residencies like this? Were we going to be up all night every night? I sure hoped not. After getting to sleep on the first night at about 3 a.m., it became very clear that we could not continue this pattern, if the two of us were going to survive. Each day we looked at each other and said only three more or two more days, which helped to keep us going.

Toward the end of the residency, I experienced what I will call a defining moment. Although most individuals were more than pleasant and genuine in their approach, and no one openly commented on my age, I experienced what I will call ageism firsthand. During one exchange, I was referred to as an "age challenged bag of hot-air." So in one short minute I felt as if my years of experience and knowledge were reduced to an insignificant level. My heart sank. I was mortified and at the same time angered that anyone would say something so hurtful. Looking back, however, this person's insensitively and rudeness actually provided me with the resolve to move forward in my quest.

"The Blizzard"

Returning from the year-one residency, my friend and I had a new resolve to move forward with course work and the development of ideas on where we wanted our dissertation journey to take us. After a year filled with work and family responsibilities, we again found ourselves in the car riding toward our year-two residency. What was ahead could only be imagined. The second in a series of three required residencies began without any real fanfare. Although I thought I had developed a tough skin after my "hot air" experience the year before, I was not quite prepared for what took place when it was my turn to present my prospectus. I really wish a friend or colleague who had traveled the doctoral road before me had shared the "so what" or "who cares" phenomenon. Being half way through and being confronted with "so what" from your faculty member is a tad disconcerting. Forewarned is forearmed, so they say, and if I had realized that the prospectus process was one in which I would be required to defend my ideas, I obviously would have been better prepared. They say all's well that ends well, but it could have been less stressful and just as educational had we been better informed.

The second residency will perhaps always be remembered more for what took place outside the classroom than in it. The blizzard of 2010 surprised not only the weatherman but me as well. With no boots, no gloves, and no real sense of humor, we found ourselves stuck in a city that all but closed down, in a hotel that was in danger of running out of food, and more than 400 miles away from family and friends. The moral of this story is to be better prepared for any eventuality. While these things can happen to anyone regardless of whether one is in school or not, it is important to remember that sometimes things happen that we don't expect and if we are to succeed in life we must always be proactive instead of reactive.

"Transformation"

The year between the second and the third residency flew by. Work, classes, family all overlapped in a whirlwind of activity. Before we knew it, Thanksgiving came, and we were packing for what had become an annual trek to residency. The longest of the residencies, a total of ten days away from home seemed daunting to say the least. What was different this time? No insults, no blizzard, and only a few late nights. Perhaps my classmates and I had adapted and learned valuable lessons during the prior residencies. Nevertheless, the year-three residency presented its own unique set of challenges.

The initial five-day course required that we work in teams to solve real world problems collaboratively. Critical self-reflection and providing constructive feedback on each of our classmates was required. A lot of time was spent thinking about where we came from, where we were, and where we were going in the future. It was at this point that I was reminded of another theory I was introduced to years earlier. Maslow's (1968) basic human needs theory provides an excellent framework for examining human action.

As individuals, we all have essential or basic needs that must be met if we are to be successful in reaching our ultimate potential; Maslow (1968) described this as self-actualization. All doctoral students, regardless of age, can benefit from a greater understanding of this theory as it applies to their personal journey. Paying attention to the basics such as food, rest, love, and family support is essential to successful completion of any degree. Remembering to take time off to be with family and decompress can go a long way when under the pressure of what seems to be constant stress and endless deadlines.

"End in Sight"

A little more than three years have passed since I returned to school. Currently, I am in the data-collection phase of my dissertation and considered ABD. Yes, that's right; I am all finished except for the dissertation. When I share this with friends and colleagues, their immediate response is, "Oh, you'll be done soon." How would they know the most difficult and often the loneliest portion of the journey are still in front of me? When I think back, I am immediately reminded of how challenged I was in those first five or six weeks of the program. I know now that many individuals presented with the same set of circumstances would have thrown in the towel. Why didn't I? Perhaps my life's experience as a nurse and an educator provided me with the needed insights to deal effectively with the situations one at a time and see them through to a successful conclusion.

The preceding story has been decades in the making. Many years ago, I decided to walk away from a doctoral program, when as a young faculty member teaching in an associate degree nursing program, I became overwhelmed by the demands of motherhood, family, and work. Thirty years later, I find myself positioned to complete the final leg of a journey by finishing the dissertation and completing my oral defense. The future is in front of me. I am hopeful that the addition of the letters EdD behind my name will open the door to many new and challenging experiences as I continue on the ultimate journey in search of greater knowledge and understanding, the journey called life.

References

Erikson, E. H. (1963). *Childhood and society* (2nd ed.). New York, NY:

    W.W. Norton & Company.

Maslow, A. H. (1968). *Toward a psychology of being* (2nd ed.). New

    York, NY: Van Nostrand Reinhold.

11 The Higher Road: My Decision to Pursue a Doctoral Degree
Carol Wells

My work experience was not pleasant. I had begun my nursing career as an LPN in a local hospital, went on to an RN upgrade program, and became licensed as an RN in 1987. I worked in medical centers, teaching hospitals, home care, and local community hospitals. I worked in high-risk specialties and really had tried, during my time in nursing, to round out my experience. I became the victim of harassment and bullying on the job, which started when I accepted an office nurse position. During that time, I went through a personal change and simultaneously lost what I saw as a great job opportunity due to internal politics. Those two events were catalysts that propelled me on my journey to remove myself from what I felt were negativity and professional restraint, which is also known as nurse bullying.

I experienced this firsthand. While I had perceived that there was some fear of job or position loss by some nursing leaders prior to this, I realized after this that nursing management and administration had basically blocked my professional accomplishments and rumors had been spread from facility to facility. Nurse bullying exists, it is ongoing, and it is a very harmful phenomena. There are many recent studies about the phenomena of nurse bullying, as this has become a very hot topic in academia worldwide. Nurse bullying can be a horizontal nurse-to-nurse issue, informal or unilateral, a planned and coordinated hostile situation, and subtle or outright. Its main goal is to ostracize and prevent the target from moving up. In a formal or coordinated act of bullying, an individual or individuals within a group map out and influence preexisting definitions of a situation (Lewis, 2006). In other words, they basically spread information or misinformation so that their target is mistreated. In nursing there is the division of labor into units. That only promotes clique formation within hospitals and other organizations, even corporate organizations. Because of the structure of a clique, there is a level of loyalty basically akin to a code of silence, in which one or another member will not allow their friends to be blamed as an instigator. This can make it hard to define who exactly is to blame for starting the bullying process.

Bullying is a very serious issue and can take the form of planning to discredit, undermine, disadvantage, and isolate; interfere in work-related practices; demean, destroy confidence, and fabricate complaints. These events can happen within a specific timeframe or may be ongoing, varying in lengths of time. Bullying can happen when a new position is created, when a promotion is to be announced, or there is a significant change in organizational structure. Although this occurs primarily within staff positions, it is not uncommon for management or administration to take part in the bullying process, which means bullying can be both horizontal and vertical (Lewis, 2006). This started for me in a small community organization, and it is my own belief that this is mostly true in these types of health organizations. It is also my experience that since nurses tend to work at several organizations, even while holding a full-time job at one, bullying can become a "cross pollination" issue. Again, this is what occurred in my case, and the perpetrators were both nurses and associated non-nursing personnel. Since nurses are subject to specialization, this creates an opportunity to form a small unit-based community, which then develops its own rules for acceptance and behavior. These communities often include associated secretarial staff and specialized technicians, who can also spend their careers in one place. Bullying can have catastrophic effects on the psyche of the victim, and many times nursing administration will make an anemic effort, at best, to do something about it. On my journey, I received little support from people around me and am still subjected to ridicule from former colleagues who did not take me seriously.

It took me a while to realize this, but my doctoral journey began years prior to beginning a doctor of health administration program of study. Since I looked for a way out of the clique situation, I began my education with a degree in health care management and then an MBA, specializing in management information systems. I then chose the on-line format for my doctorate because prior to deciding to return for my doctorate, I had returned for additional MBA specialties, which I also did on-line. This new format was very intriguing for me since my previous education was achieved in traditional programs. I was really impressed with the self-directed learning modality and enjoyed the additional research we accomplished during each class. I also enjoyed writing papers and participating in discussions. In this particular MBA program, we had group projects and had to meet in chat rooms to discuss our projects as part of the course. At least once or twice during the course section, our facilitators conducted discussions in chat rooms to review material or assignments. I had researched a number of on-line doctoral programs; I applied to the University of Phoenix (UOP) in the summer of 2006 but did not begin studies there until late spring of 2007. I love that UOP is so technologically advanced, that the university focuses on the business model of health services, and that the faculty remains current on health policy.

I had spoken to a couple of other nurses on social networks who also had been subjected to bullying and also left their specializations or left nursing entirely because of it. In fact, just before I accepted my ill-fated position, I had been speaking to a physician whose wife worked on the same unit I had worked on, and who felt bullied enough that she also left. Jackson, Clare, and Mannix (2002), indicated research suggests "there is evidence that increasing numbers of nursing and other health professionals are suffering the effects of post-traumatic stress disorder, anxiety, impaired work performance, and difficulties with sleep as a result of hostility and violence in the workplace" (p. 14). Studies also suggested a direct correlation between aggression, sick leave, burnout, and staff turnover. Very often, there is a blame-the-victim mentality among aggressors, who do not wish to take responsibility for their actions. When colleagues actively bully a person, the result can mean a loss of confidence and fear of reprisal; this makes it difficult for that individual to speak up (Lewis, 2006). Imagine what it means when managers and administrators participate.

An embedded organization is one that has existed for a long time and typically functions within a small geographic area. Embedded organizations often do not move beyond the basic competition model and therefore tend to stagnate. These organizations usually hire from the same community and tend to promote from within. Geographic areas may have a number of hospitals that cross personnel and are culturally similar. This creates a means for a usual model of behavior or practice methodology to flourish. If the same people are working in

110

organizations for a number of years, it is doubtful new ideas are

entering the culture or new and different personnel are joining the

workforce. Most of the personnel stay on for the length of their

careers, and it becomes very difficult to change the internal culture

of an embedded organization.

Organizational climate is how personnel perceive

organizational policy, method of performing their duties, and the

mechanism of how they move up within the organization and reach

professional or personal goals. The climate of an organization

largely shapes the outlook of its personnel. The structure of the

organization, meaning its overall personnel and management

structure, shapes the employees' behavior, perceptions, and

attitudes (Schein, 1996). Organizations evolve to become akin to

small communities, and the way personnel behave is how they

collectively have learned to deal with external influences, including

those that may be perceived as threatening or competitive.

Organizational culture is similar to ethnic culture in that it also has

social mores of acceptable behavior, unacceptable behavior, and

ritualized behavior. According to Sleutel (2000), Schein

conceptualized that "culture and subcultures exist within

organizational structures" (pp. 2-3). Within the nursing culture, which is a large part of the healthcare environment, behaviors are both individualized and group-based. Nursing has its own culture and unit-based subcultures, which blend with the nonmedical workforce, the managerial workforce, and overall organization executives.

In historical approaches to the nursing profession, there were not many opportunities that existed outside of direct patient care and direct nursing management or administration. It was easier to make someone look bad if it seemed someone could lose an opportunity or needed to protect a job. Newcomers were threatening if they could bring in alternate methods of performing job functions, were competent, or had achieved higher education. This is where existing employees closed ranks. Further, it appears to me that as soon as the perception of a situation is let out of the bag, anything you do is suspect; those who feel threatened meet everything you do to move forward with suspicion and subsequently participate in bullying. Even now, it seems that autonomy in the nursing profession is poor. Because of the rumor mill that followed me, I went through many cycles of unemployment and underemployment and had difficulty, even with my education, in finding work outside of patient care. In fact, I could not find work at all that did not mean shift work on a patient care unit. When I finally had the opportunity to change that, I did, even though it meant I would be unemployed for a period of time. I trained first as a legal nurse consultant, became a member of the specialty organization, contributed to their professional journal, and then became a paralegal. I refused just to have a paycheck, to be dragged (as I call it) back into a cycle of employment, underemployment, and unemployment that would not benefit me.

My reason for going for my doctorate was to cap off my study in management and administration within the health care sector. I knew I did not want to return to patient care nursing. There still seemed to be the belief I would give up and come back to reality (floor nursing, patient care, or some aspect of it), but I lost interest in those years ago. The legal side of healthcare and health policy administration is very interesting to me, especially its impact on the healthcare environment, and I have seen that with my education and background, there are other options. Health policy has been an interest of mine for a long time, and it was one of the specialties I had considered prior to applying to UOP. Employment within the health environment and its associated specialties owes a lot to the understanding of the intricate balance between the work environment and health policy. Because this balance includes the direct effect on the health of the consumer, factors such as global health systems and population health are also significant. Because of the mix of private and public health payers in this country, how these affect the health process in total requires an understanding of the business aspect. Health law is dynamic, and health policy is ever changing. I feel that I am now in a very good place. I will not continue to place myself in a situation where the use of rumors and speculation deny me autonomy in my future. I have seen that my role has expanded beyond that.

A return to the university to complete my education is appealing to me, and what I love about the on-line process is that it is so convenient and technically up to date. At the onset of the doctoral process, authorship of a dissertation seems daunting, but as we learn in our residencies, it doesn't have to be. During my dissertation process, I accumulated an abundance of research in a subject that had interested me for years. The fact that I had so much information meant that I was cross-referencing, which was intentional, but which made the paper appear unfocused. When I contacted the person who was to be my mentor, what I liked was that he was working in one of the areas I was researching. I thought this would be a bonus because he would have first-hand knowledge of the subject. However, I eventually had difficulty getting in touch with him, and we had disagreements about methodology. This meant completing my dissertation was taking a long time. I also felt the residency had not fully addressed the dissertation process, and this led to feeling I was not getting direction from my mentor or support from the university. Since I was looking at my dissertation in terms of an in-depth study, this probably meant I was focusing too much on *what* I was trying to write instead of just focusing on *how* to write the paper. I realize that the dissertation is supposed to be a cumulative reflection of the knowledge and scholarship gained through the doctoral process, but in retrospect, my approach was far too complicated.

Finally, in addition to difficulties professionally and then with the dissertation process, I developed health issues that kept me away from my studies and prevented me from actively

participating in class. At that point I decided it was better to take a

break and restart the process when I was ready. I felt this was the

right decision because I would then be able to basically start fresh

with the process and devote time to my dissertation with a new

topic and new mentor. The importance of being organized can and

does assist in structuring the process, and I am fortunate to realize

what my mistakes were the first time. I am looking forward to a

new team of advisors and restarting my dissertation. I also had to

take stock of where I was and what I could conceivably do

professionally in the future, long term. I explored the possibility of

stepping back into an MSN—yes, nursing—at UOP with a

nonclinical specialty. I have some background in case management

and education, both staff and patient-based, and had a brief stint as

a university-level adjunct. I enjoy teaching; that one aspect of the

PhD interested me greatly, and I would like to revisit it in the

future.

At this point, I am still dealing with health issues. My

decision and commitment to return to my studies are on hold,

although I maintain communication with my doctoral advisor. I have tried to keep abreast of the changes in health care by blogging (http://leftistmoderatespeak.wordpress.com) and reading blogs. I find social media can put us in touch with many people who can assist us in our journey. The newly revised UOP E-Campus Forum is a great addition, and the diversity of people at the university makes it a very engaging experience. The Internet offers so many opportunities for anyone to find subjects to learn from.

References

Jackson, D., Clare, J., & Mannix, J. (2002). Who would want to be a nurse? Violence in the workplace: A factor in recruitment and retention. *Journal of Nursing Management, 10,* 13-20.

Lewis, M. A. (2006). Nurse bullying: Organizational considerations in the maintenance and perpetration of health care bullying cultures. *Journal of Nursing Management, 14*(1), 52-58.

Schein, E. H. (1996). Culture: The missing concept in organization studies. *Administrative Science Quarterly, 41*(2), 1-10.

Sleutel, M. (2000). Climate, culture, context, or work environment? Organizational factors that influence nursing practice. *Journal of Nursing Administration, 30*(2), 53-59.

12 Pursuing a Doctoral Degree: Why Did I Do It?

Beth B. Williams

I have always been a firm believer in, and proponent of, the benefits of education. During the 1980s, I was a nontraditional student well before universities realized what a nontraditional student was all about. In 1982, I graduated with a two-year degree and went to work full-time. During an 8-year span of 16-hour days, and 130-mile round trips, plus going through my first pregnancy, I managed to complete my bachelor's degree. I still remember meeting with an advisor at the main campus of the university after he examined my final transcript. He said, "How did you do all of this while working full-time and having a baby. Are you still sane?" Remember there was no Internet. I had to take a day of vacation to register for classes, and believe me it was not a vacation! After graduation, I worked for a few years without thoughts of pursuing any further degrees. After all, I had to recover from the years of taking it one day at a time!

But within a few years the educational itch returned, and I considered obtaining an MBA. During this period, some quality universities offered MBA classes at satellite schools. I was ecstatic at the idea of not having to drive hundreds of miles to classes. At this time, there was still no Internet widely available, but the use of the fax machine and telephone registration made the off-site concept work fairly smoothly. The essence of the master's program was focused on total quality control and teamwork. Working with other learners who all worked full-time in careers, was challenging and invigorating. I enjoyed the challenges and could apply what I learned immediately in my workplace. My brain was not only absorbing the knowledge to enhance my skills and abilities, but the knowledge improved processes and procedures within my organization. During my last class for the MBA program, I skipped one class to deliver my second child! After that came graduation.

After completing the MBA degree, I was done, completely finished with the educational path forever! I had no desire or need to pursue an advanced doctoral degree because the monetary rewards or the workplace incentives did not seem to exist. In my current career I advanced rapidly and enjoyed the rewards that

120

came with it. My employer provided the growth opportunities necessary to use all the skills I learned in my management classes and rewarded me with monetary benefits.

Over the next decade, my organization experienced extreme growth in revenues and employees. Our employee base doubled and gave me many challenging moments. Some of the moments were extremely stressful but the hands-on management experiences provided a great way to learn and grow as a supervisor. I found out just how thrilling and exasperating it is to supervise and mentor employees who often have issues that complicate their working behaviors. The knowledge we get from school does little to prepare us for the realities of dealing with the eccentricities of fallible human employees. My most memorable hire came with the provision added by myself, "Of course we have a flexible workplace." Boy, did I ever eat those words!

I immediately learned it is better sometimes to not give an inch at the beginning of employment because some individuals assume they can take miles! Within a month of hire, the employee had to be reprimanded (by myself, of course) because of making international calls. I assumed the issue was resolved, and our happy workplace would resume and progress. Within two months, the same employee was not meeting deadlines and violating our personal telephone policy. Again, I had a heart-to-heart talk with the individual in hopes of making a bad situation better. To make a long story short, within nine months I got to experience having to let someone go for poor performance. Try getting *that* experience in school!

My workplace began to experience decline during 2006-2007. The director allowed dysfunction to exist between various executives. Staff morale declined, and eventually we had to reduce our staff by 30%. The frustration I experienced was because of not having any control over the other executive's dysfunctional behavior. My recommendations to the director went unheeded. So what did I have control over?

The question of lack of control was on my mind, and after discussing the issue with my husband; he suggested an idea that at first I thought was preposterous. He said, "Why not go back to school and improve yourself?" My mind came up with all the valid reasons I couldn't do something like that. Some of the reasons were the cost of education, the time investment, and the fact that I had been out of school for so long, and of course whether I had the desire to take on such a lofty goal. I mulled this over for a few weeks. Searching on the Internet, I found many accredited universities that offered various doctoral degrees on-line. On-line education sounded intriguing.

I went on the Internet and filled out on-line applications to find out more information for three universities. By the time I was done and had walked downstairs my phone was ringing. It was one of the universities returning my inquiry! "Wow, that is great customer service," I thought. With some trepidation, I chose the university with such prompt customer service, hoping their academic offerings would be as responsive as their marketing. After talking with an advisor and figuring out all the technicalities of the process, I started my doctoral journey.

I enjoyed the on-line classroom immensely. I have a strong computer science background, so I felt quite comfortable in the on-line element. The classes were demanding but enjoyable, taught by professionals who had real-world experience. The only issue I had was what subject matter to do my dissertation on? I did not have a "passion," and I did not feel driven toward any particular topic.

My advisor, the professors, and the other learners assured me the subject would come to me in time.

And in time I did manage to find a topic that was not only realistic but grabbed me where it needed. I still struggled with the writing, but eventually the ideas and themes began to pull together in a coherent manner. What I discovered during the journey was how important the people we come in contact with are in helping to complete the journey successfully. My family gave me the time I needed, my professors provided the fodder, my mentor encouraged and cheered me throughout the process, and the other learners were both empathetic and supportive. During four years of many late nights, there were many stressful times where I thought I would never complete the dissertation process. But I hung in there and got through one day or night at a time.

Now I reflect and ask, "Why did I pursue a doctoral degree?" The answer is one that I would not have given when I started the journey. Perhaps hindsight makes one wiser. Or perhaps the experiences during the journey changed my perspective. But the only answer to the question, at least for me, is that I did for it for *me* and *me* alone. No matter what happens in my life after this achievement, I will always have the experience of reaching for the highest educational degree possible, grasping the concepts and making them mine. No one can ever take that from me.

About the Authors

Rose Marie Balan, Ed.D.

Rose Marie Balan was born and raised in Manitoba, on the Canadian prairie. After graduating from university, she started her teaching career in the village of Ethelbert, which at that time had a population of slightly more than 450 people. After three years, she moved to British Columbia to be nearer to her family. In all, she has been a classroom teacher for 34 years, and has always taught in the primary grades. Her passions include: learning, researching, reading, and traveling. Rose Marie considers herself to be a lifelong learner. She retired from classroom teaching in July 2011, but is eager to move on to other options. Rose Marie hopes to teach at the university level so she can share what she has learned through her recent studies and classroom experiences.

****

Edith Caldwell

Edith Caldwell has an associate degree in applied business, a bachelor's in computer science (information technology), and a master's in organizational management. She has worked in corporate America for over 40 years. Edith is employed in administration at a university in the College of Engineering. She is pursuing a doctorate in educational leadership from the University of Phoenix.

****

Gabriel Flores, Ed.D.

Gabriel Flores has a doctor of education in educational leadership and 15 years of classroom experience within the Los Angeles Unified School District (LAUSD). His interests include qualitative research and the inclusion of sexual orientation education within multicultural education programs. Gabriel currently works as an adjunct faculty member in the College of Education at University of Phoenix.

****

Amanda Grihm

Amanda Grihm was born in Youngstown, Ohio. At the age of nine her mother remarried and moved her and her younger brother, Terry, to Cleveland, Ohio. She is the eighth of nine children. Amanda currently resides in Stone Mountain, GA. She is an entrepreneur, author, playwright, nonprofit executive, and a consummate service-oriented professional. Amanda has always used story creation and story listening as tools to illuminate and work through problems in the various fields she has worked including customer service, case management, consulting, events management, human resources, marketing, and training and development. She is a creative person and innovative problem-solver.

Amanda enjoys the arts, and specifically, the art of storytelling. She is a highly skilled story creator and story listener. She founded a new form of consulting called corporate playacting. Her stories and programs all have creative solutions that resolve long-standing problems others find difficult to comprehend and solve.

After writing her novel, *The Wolf*, in 2002 she found that writing was a tool that could improve personal organizational skills, logic and critical analysis. Because of this realization she produced a creative workshop and program, *Reaching through Readings and Writing* (RTRW). Amanda presented her RTRW workshop as teacher development training for middle-school teachers in DeKalb

County, GA. She also presented six-week RTRW workshops at detention centers and shelters in Georgia.

Amanda' s biological father died, homeless, when she was a baby. Homelessness has always been a battle that Amanda has chosen to fight. In 1992, she founded and ran Project Match, Incorporated, a 501(c) 3 nonprofit corporation that matched homeless single-parent families with senior and disabled citizens who lived alone. Along with her husband, J. Emil, Amanda ran Project Match for 13 years. Later Amanda wrote and produced a full-length play, *Going Home*, a dramatic comedy about a female executive who becomes homeless and ultimately finds a way to end homelessness for a small segment of the homeless population. The play brings attention to some of the real problems associated with homelessness such as a) the homelessness of women and children, b) the alienation of disabled and senior citizens who live alone, and c) the lack of resources to address the issues that keep people homeless.

Amanda is nearly finished with her doctor of education in educational technology. In her doctoral studies, Amanda is focused on the impact that digital storytelling may have on learned helpless students. Learned helplessness is a condition in which people who have faced so many adversities start to believe that they are incapable of achieving success. Amanda thinks these beliefs represent illogically conceived perceptions, and in reality there are no barriers to success.

Amanda's latest venture finds her still using storytelling to illuminate the root cause of problems. She recently launched a new consultancy under Amanda Grihm Enterprises, LLC, in which she conducts corporate playacting workshops to help managers take a holistic view of some of the problems they encounter. The workshops also illustrate instances of learned helplessness, among other problems in the workforce.

****

Carla Hill

Carla Hill is a teaching associate in mathematics at Marist College in Poughkeepsie, NY. Over the summer she also teaches in the Upward Bound program through Marist. Carla has been an adjunct lecturer at Dutchess Community College since January, 1980 and started as an adjunct at Marist in 2000 and is now full-time. She grew up in Southeast Washington, D.C. and after living there for 18 years went to rural North Carolina for college. She holds a bachelor's in mathematics from Lenoir Rhyne University in Hickory, NC. Carla completed one year of graduate work in computer science at Clemson University in Clemson, SC before moving to the Poughkeepsie area and completing her master's in computer science at Union College in Schenectady, NY.

She decided to continue for her doctorate after over 30 years because she wanted to find ways to better serve her students, especially those students with learning disabilities. Her program is the doctor of education in educational leadership with a specialization in educational technology because she believes in the use of technology as an aid to traditional teaching. Carla has taught a class on-line for the past six years during the regular semester and summer session. She recently went through the on-line course re-design institute to bring the course up to the national quality matters standards. Carla feels the on-line format of the University of Phoenix will help her understand the challenges her students face in an on-line course.

Outside of work, Carla has two grown children and three grandchildren. She is involved in Girl Scouts as an assistant leader for a Cadette Troop and a council trainer. She is a certified First Aid and CPR/AED instructor and maintains her own certifications. Carla also judge's women's gymnastics, both high school and club. For relaxation she likes to read, work Sudoku puzzles, watch TV - usually while reading or doing puzzles - check in with her friends on Facebook and attend Marist athletics competitions – go Red Foxes!

****

Trina Moskalik

Trina Moskalik lives outside of Milwaukee, Wisconsin with her husband, daughter, and two dogs. She is pursuing her doctor of management in organizational leadership with a graduation date of summer, 2013. Her pursuit of lifelong learning comes in many forms including formal education, professional seminars, a myriad of hobbies, and avid reading.

****

Karen F. Phillips, Ed.D.

Karen F. Phillips was born and raised in northeastern Pennsylvania. She received her baccalaureate degree from Misericordia University (1976), master's from University of Phoenix

(2004) and doctor of education from University of Phoenix (2010) with a concentration in curriculum and instruction. In 1983, Karen married her husband Ken. They have three children: Marc (25), Cara (22) and Ryan (20) as well as two dogs, Harvey and Possum. Karen has taught in various nursing programs on an LPN, associate, baccalaureate, and graduate levels. Currently, she is an assistant professor of nursing at William Paterson University (Wayne, NJ).

Education has always played a powerful role in Karen's life. Coining a phrase from Sir Francis Bacon, she believes "knowledge is power and education is the key to success." Learning should be life long to remain a dynamic force in both education and nursing. Her belief is that being a lifelong learner is vital to becoming an effective educator and leader. Karen has been a nurse for 35 years, primarily in the maternal child area and is also a certified lactation consultant and childbirth educator. She has presented her research in several forums in New Jersey and the Sigma Theta Tau International Biennial Conference in Texas. In her spare time, Karen enjoys reading, researching, traveling, relaxing with friends and family, and volunteering in her community.

****

Holly Rick, Ph.D.

Holly Rick graduated with her PhD in organizational management specializing in leadership in 2009. She holds an MBA and a bachelor degree in business administration-finance. She is currently a student at the University of Arizona working towards a master's in information and library science. Her expected graduation date is 2012.

****

George W. Rideout, D.B.A.

George W. Rideout is a principal for Evolution Strategists LLC and executive director of the Change Leadership Intelligence (CLQ) Institute. He holds an MBA and numerous professional certifications, including the certified six sigma black belt (CSSBB), and the FCIB international certified credit executive (ICCE). George is a published author and frequent speaker, with more than 16 years' experience in sales and management, leading sales teams in the United States and Canada. His research interests include change leadership, decision-making, leadership studies, multiple intelligences, and systems theories.

****

Carl Schwander

Staff Sergeant Carl Schwander serves on active duty with the United States Army Field Artillery. He holds a master of public administration from the University of Phoenix and currently is pursuing his doctorate in organizational leadership. Carl is married to Katelyn Schwander and is the proud father of two daughters, Sara and Chelsey.

****

Mary J. Stedman

Mary J. Stedman is a professor and associate chairperson, for the Department of Nursing at Farmingdale Sate College in Farmingdale, New York. She has more than 30 years of experience in nursing, the majority of which has been spent educating student nurses at the associate degree level. She currently teaches in both the generic baccalaureate nursing program and the RN to BS completion program. Professor Stedman has been singled out for excellence in teaching and was the recipient of the State University of New York Chancellors Award for Excellence in Teaching in 2003. Professor Stedman was a member of the New York State Task Force on Educational Mobility, which was instrumental in developing the

LPN to RN Articulation Model still in use today. She continues to serve on statewide initiatives related to education and nursing and is an active member of the Council of Associate Degree Nursing Education.

A leader in nursing education, Professor Stedman has been an active member of the National League for Nursing, serving as an elected member of the Nurse Educator Workforce Development Advisory Council. During her tenure as chair of this council issues concerning faculty compensation, faculty mentoring, and healthful work environments were highlighted. Professor Stedman is a frequent presenter on topics related to nursing education and career mobility on the local, state and national level. She decided to pursue her doctorate to complete an unfinished journey she had abandoned years earlier and to serve as a role model to her younger faculty colleagues.

****

Carol Wells

Carol Wells graduated with an associate degree in nursing in 1987, baccalaureate degree in health care management in 1999, and master of business administration specializing in management information systems in 2001. She then returned to an on-line program for two additional MBA specialties in health care management & marketing, which she completed in 2005. Because of an unexpected illness Carol had to put her doctoral studies on hold, but plans to resume in the near future. She has also completed a paralegal program. Carol's work as a nurse has included working in several specialties and types of nursing, administrative/supervisor capacities, and in several types of health care organizations, including hospital medical centers, long-term care, home care, and physician offices.

****

Beth B. Williams, D.M.

Beth B. Williams has an extensive background in computer science working as a system analyst in both the private and public sector. Initially her career started in research and development in the weapons industry working in software engineering for weapons systems. Beth worked on many large-scale projects for both the department of defense and private contractors. She left that industry during the recession of the 1980s and worked in the software industry for private accounting firms. Beth collaborated and supervised programming teams for various accounting software packages sold to third party firms. During the last 20 years she has moved into managing governmental work supervising information technology, business, and financial staff. The main focus of Beth's current work is managing various types of projects including rehabilitative housing, vocational rehabilitative services, and fund-based financial management. Beth is married with two children. She and her husband have established and run many business ventures over the years.

www.ingramcontent.com/pod-product-compliance
Lightning Source LLC
Chambersburg PA
CBHW061729020426
42331CB00006B/1163